Bible Gems

SCRIPTURE VERSES ON GOD'S MERCY AND OVERCOMING FEAR

DONALD H. CALLOWAY, MIC

Available from:
Marian Helpers Center
Stockbridge, MA 01263

Prayerline: 1-800-804-3823
Orderline: 1-800-462-7426
Websites: FatherCalloway.com
Marian.org

Imprimi Potest:
Very Rev. Chris Alar, MIC
Provincial Superior
The Blessed Virgin Mary, Mother of Mercy Province
July 31, 2023
Feast of St. Ignatius of Loyola

Nihil Obstat:
Robert A. Stackpole, STD
Censor Deputatus
July 31, 2023

ISBN: 978-1-59614-598-6
Library of Congress Control Number: 2023943093

Printed in the United States of America

Do not be afraid.
Open wide the doors
for Christ.

– POPE ST. JOHN PAUL II

INTRODUCTION

Bible Gems is the sixth book in the *Gems* series from Marian Press: *Marian Gems, Rosary Gems, St. Joseph Gems, Eucharistic Gems,* and *Sacred Heart Gems.* The idea behind the series is to offer a reflection and inspirational thought on a particular theme for each day of the year.

The response to the *Gems* series has been very positive. As I travel and speak at parishes and conferences throughout the U.S.A., as well as internationally, many people have told me that they appreciate the series, have made it a part of their morning routine, and continue to reflect on the "gem" throughout the day.

In recent times, people around the world are experiencing a renewed interest in participating in programs that offer reflections on the Sacred Scriptures. It is wonderful to witness so many people encountering the Word of God. At one point, the #1 rated podcast in the United States was *The Bible in a Year* by Fr. Mike Schmitz; since its inception, the podcast has been repeatedly in the top 10 of all Apple podcasts. Something extraordinary is happening!

Why such an interest in the Word of God in our times? Perhaps it is because the world in which we live is filled with much anxiety, fear, and worry. It can't be denied that the various global crises that have taken place in the last several years have put everyone on edge and increased stress levels in individuals, families, and society at large.

What could be better than to look to the Word of God for comfort, strength, and hope?

With this in mind, we decided to publish *Bible Gems: Scripture Verses on God's Mercy and Overcoming Fear.* By "we" I mean myself, the Association of Marian Helpers (AMH), and Marian Press. Thanks to Dr. Joe McAleer and Chris Sparks, what was initially a project done for TheDivineMercy.org developed into the idea for another book in the *Gems* series. Chris Sparks did the grunt work of selecting the passages from Scripture, as well as writing the daily reflections. Once the entire series was completed online, everything was passed on to me so that I could edit each entry and reflection so that it could be put into book form. It was a collaborative effort, and I am very grateful for the humble assistance of Dr. McAleer and the hard work of Chris Sparks.

As you will note, the selected passages from Scripture follow the biblical timeline from Genesis to Revelation. This was done so that the reader is not bouncing around from one book of the Bible to another in random fashion. The overarching theme of the biblical gems within is God's mercy, overcoming fear, and the Divine Mercy spirituality of trust. The brief reflection that follows each Scripture passage is meant to give hope to the reader and convey a message of confidence in God.

What the world needs right now is the assurance that God has a plan and is trustworthy, even when everything around us seems to be falling apart. By living a Divine Mercy spirituality of trust, we do not have to be afraid of the evil times in which we live. "Do not be afraid," perhaps the most well-known phrase of the pontificate of Pope St. John Paul II, comes across very strongly in the daily reflections. It is a message that is timeless and brings comfort to the heart.

The most important thing to be taken away from this book is that God loves you. He has not forgotten or abandoned you. He knows your situation, hardships, and struggles. He wants to comfort you, offer hope, and assure you that He is loving, trustworthy, and merciful. My prayer is that this little book helps you to know and experience that message.

For anyone who wants to read the entire Bible from the vantage point of a Divine Mercy spirituality, I highly recommend obtaining a copy of the *Divine Mercy Catholic Bible*. A joint publication of Ascension Press and the Marian Fathers, it looks at the Scriptures through the lens of God's merciful love and contains insights, commentary, and reflections from the saints, Church documents, the Marian Fathers, and people who work with the Marian Fathers in spreading the Divine Mercy message and devotion.

Do not be afraid! Trust in the mercy and love of Jesus.

Very Rev. Donald H. Calloway, MIC, STL
Vicar Provincial, Marian Fathers of the Immaculate Conception of the B.V.M., Blessed Virgin Mary, Mother of Mercy Province

JANUARY

January 1

**The word of the LORD came to Abram in a vision:
"Do not fear, Abram! I am your shield;
your reward shall be very great."**
GENESIS 15:1

Much of the Old Testament is the story of God retraining
fallen mankind to say (and believe) "God, I trust in You!"
Because of his faithful response to God and God's
promises, Abram becomes Abraham, our father in faith
(see Rom 3:27-4:25).

January 2

God heard the voice of the lad, and the angel of God called to Hagar from heaven. And said to her, "What troubles you, Hagar? Fear not; for God has heard the voice of the lad where he is."

Genesis 21:17

Even though Ishmael was not the child of God's covenantal promise to Abraham, God still loved him and took care of him. God hears the voices of all children in need, even if we don't see those prayers answered in this life.

January 3

The LORD appeared to [Isaac] the same night and said: "I am the God of Abraham your father; fear not, for I am with you and will bless you and multiply your descendants for my servant Abraham's sake."

Genesis 26:24

God provides for Isaac, Abraham's son of the promise, so abundantly that there is more than enough water for Isaac's household and the shepherds of the area. Just so does God provide infinite grace to all those in the household of the New Isaac, Jesus Christ, the Divine Mercy Incarnate.

January 4

[Jacob said,] "Let us arise and go up to Bethel, that I may make an altar to the God who answered me in the day of my distress and has been with me wherever I have gone."
GENESIS 35:3

Surrender your idols, as Jacob and his household did.
Put God first, family second, self third. Put not your trust
in princes and power, or money and earthly security, or
health and pleasure.

January 5

**[Joseph said,] "Rest assured, do not be afraid;
your God and the God of your father must have put
treasure in your sacks for you."**
GENESIS 43:23

The patriarch Joseph was secretly providing for his family,
even though his brothers had done him grievous harm.
We, too, can live the Golden Rule (see Mt 7:12), both
being merciful to those who have done wrong to us and
still loving ourselves, protecting ourselves from the harm
they may seek to do us.

January 6

"I am God, the God of your father; do not be afraid to go down to Egypt; for I will there make of you a great nation."
GENESIS 46:3

God called Jacob, whom He had renamed Israel, to go with his family to be strangers in a strange land, promising that they would all return home one day. God is with us wherever we are, and His mercy endures forever.

January 7

[Joseph said to his brothers,] "You meant evil against me; but God meant it for good, to bring it about that many people should be kept alive, as they are today."
GENESIS 50:20

Through the betrayal of his brothers, the patriarch Joseph found himself in Egypt at just the right time and in just the right circumstances to rise to power, becoming second in command after Pharaoh — and thus he was in the right place at the right time to store up enough food to save the known world from starvation. Truly, God's ways are not our ways, and He can bring good even out of the evils we face in life, especially if we remain obedient to His will, as Joseph did (see Rom 8:28).

January 8

Moses said to the people, "Fear not, stand firm, and see the salvation of the LORD, which he will work for you today; for the Egyptians whom you see today, you shall never see again. The LORD will fight for you, and you have only to be still."

EXODUS 14:13-14

As Pharaoh and his forces pursued the Israelites, Moses reassured the Chosen People that God had their backs. God can win a victory even when it seems impossible, if we are persistent in our trust in Him.

January 9

Moses said to the people, "Do not fear; for God has come to test you, and that fear of him may be before your eyes, that you may not sin."

EXODUS 20:20

"The beginning of wisdom is fear of the Lord" (Prov 9:10): Throughout the Old Testament, God helps mankind recover from the fall of Adam and Eve by making covenants with His Chosen People and giving them the Law. In the Ten Commandments, God is training all mankind once again in truth, faithful love of God and neighbor, and obedience to goodness.

January 10

[The LORD said,] "My presence will go with you, and I will give you rest."

EXODUS 33:14

God is the Creator of everything, and is present to us and all powerful everywhere. There are no limits to His ability to help us; we can rest in the surety of His love and providential care.

January 11

[The LORD said,] "I will give peace in the land, and you will shall lie down, and none shall make you afraid; and I will remove evil beasts from the land, and the sword shall not go through your land."
LEVITICUS 26:6

God, Who is also Truth and Goodness, guarantees to the Israelites that there are consequences to living according to the natural law and to the truth. Goodness brings about good things, prosperity, and peace; as Pope St. Paul VI famously said, "If you want peace, work for justice."

January 12

[Joshua and Caleb said,] "Only, do not rebel against the LORD; and do not fear the people of the land, for they are bread for us; their protection is removed from them, and the LORD is with us; do not fear them."

NUMBERS 14:9

Going where God calls us to go and doing what He summons us to do through our vocations, our personal charisms (gifts of the Holy Spirit), or through lawful instructions from the Church and those with legitimate authority over us can seem scary. But God will make a way, even where it seems dangerous or impossible, for God is our Good Shepherd (see Ps 23).

January 13

The LORD said to Moses, "Do not fear [Og, king of Bashan]; for I have given him into your hand, and all his people, and his land; and you shall do to him as you did to Sihon, king of the Amorites, who dwelt at Heshbon."

NUMBERS 21:34

Earthly powers can seem impossible to confront or to overcome, but God is greater than any king or earthly authority. We can with certainty pray, "Jesus, I trust in You!"

January 14

[Moses said], "You shall not be partial in judgment; you shall hear the small and the great alike; you shall not be afraid of the face of man, for the judgment is God's; and the case that is too hard for you, you shall bring to me, and I will hear it."

DEUTERONOMY 1:17

When we have a job or other responsibilities, we can be assured that God is on the side of doing that job well, according to justice, prudence, and the rest of the virtues. We need have no fear, even in the face of real negative consequences for doing the job right: God will be our ultimate vindication and support.

January 15

[Moses said], "Behold, the Lord your God has set the land before you; go up, take possession, as the Lord, the God of your fathers, has told you; do not fear or be dismayed."

DEUTERONOMY 1:21

God brought the Israelites to the Promised Land, but out of fear, the people did not believe their scouts' positive reports, ultimately dooming them to wander the desert for 40 more years. Don't make the same mistake! Live the spirituality of "Jesus, I trust in You!"

January 16

[Moses said,] "Do not be in dread or afraid of them. The Lord your God who goes before you will himself fight for you, just as he did for you in Egypt before your eyes."

DEUTERONOMY 1:29-30

No matter the difficulties we face, if we are faithfully following God's call and trying to be obedient to His will, Providence will govern our lives, not the ways of the world, the corruption of the flesh, or the malice of the devil. Abide in the Holy Spirit and watch God work.

January 17

From Aroer, which is on the edge of the valley of the Arnon, and from the city that is in the valley, as far as Gilead, there was not a city too high for us; the LORD our God gave all into our hands.

DEUTERONOMY 2:36

When we go where God calls us and set our hands to the tasks He gives us, we will work with supernatural strength. We will do impossible things, for all things are possible with God (see Mt 19:26).

January 18

The LORD said to [Moses], "Do not fear [Og, king of Bashan]; for I have given him and all his people and his land into your hand; and you shall do to him as you did to Sihon king of the Amorites, who dwelt at Heshbon."

DEUTERONOMY 3:2

When we trust God and seek to make our will match His, we place ourselves on the side of the power that sustains the cosmos. Stand with God! Sometimes, you will be granted the privilege to see His providence ordering the world around you; the rest of the time, you can know for sure that His providence will ultimately prevail.

January 19

[Moses said,] "Do not fear them, for it is the LORD your God who fights for you."
DEUTERONOMY 3:22

Even when we must share the Passion of Jesus, our Lord, we can know we will see ultimate victory either in this life or the next. Do not be afraid of anyone or anything, not even death, because God is greater than all.

January 20

[Moses said,] "You shall not be afraid of them, but you shall remember what the LORD your God did to Pharaoh and to all Egypt."
DEUTERONOMY 7:18

The Lord God laid waste to the gods of the Egyptians and demonstrated that earthly power is nothing compared to His own. Do not be afraid of the enemies of Goodness, Truth, and Beauty; our God is greater.

January 21

**[Moses said,] "You shall not be in dread of them;
for the LORD your God is in the midst of you,
a great and terrible God."**

DEUTERONOMY 7:21

We can forget that the One who quietly, constantly
holds everything in existence is so incredibly powerful,
because the greatest strength is also often most subtle,
most precise, and most easily overlooked. But God is in
our midst, even as so many people mistake His immense
power for powerlessness. God is with us; so long as we are
also with God, of whom should we be afraid?

January 22

[Moses said,] "When you go forth to war against your enemies, and see horses and chariots and an army larger than your own, you shall not be afraid of them; for the LORD your God is with you, who brought you up out of the land of Egypt."

DEUTERONOMY 20:1

By nature, we are weak, with excessive or unruly desires, perceiving the truth with difficulty, and struggling in this valley of tears. But by grace, all things are possible — so stick close to the Lord and see what He will do, even in the face of mighty foes!

January 23

[Moses said,] "Hear, O Israel, you draw near this day to battle against your enemies: let not your heart faint; do not fear, tremble, or be in dread of them."

DEUTERONOMY 20:3

As we are on pilgrimage through life, we will, like Jesus, encounter enemies. So long as we remain in God's love and remain alive in the Spirit, we can confront these enemies with God's own love and the courage, the Heart, of Christ Himself.

January 24

[Moses said,] "We cried to the LORD the God of our fathers, and the LORD heard our voice, and saw our affliction, our toil and our oppression."

DEUTERONOMY 26:7

For all that human history is full of oppression and evil, it is also full of stories of unlikely heroes and divine intervention, of times where Heaven's hand can be detected in the overthrow of injustice, such as in the life and works of St. Joan of Arc (ca. 1412-1431), Pope St. John Paul II (1920-2005), and many other heroes of our faith. Let us cry out to God on behalf of the oppressed, set to work in pursuit of justice and mercy in the world, and by our faithful Catholic witness, help transform our times and communities.

January 25

[Moses said,] **"Be strong and of good courage; do not fear or dread of them, for it is the Lord, your God, who marches with you; he will never fail you or forsake you."**
DEUTERONOMY 31:6

God will never fail or forsake us, even if we fail or forsake Him through sin or lack of trust. We can't overcome the evils or brokenness of this world on our own strength, but by God's grace and with God, we can be strong and steadfast; we are able to have no fear or dread of anything that is not God.

January 26

**Then Moses summoned Joshua, and said to him in the
sight of all Israel, "Be strong and of good courage; for
you shall go with bring this people into the land which
the LORD has sworn to their fathers to give them; and you
shall put them in possession of it."**

DEUTERONOMY 31:7

The Church's tradition includes the notion of "graces
of state," or the grace God gives us so we can fulfill the
responsibilities of our vocation. We are not given spouses,
or children, or work to do on earth without being
equipped to do the will of God in these walks of life; if we
prudently discern what we are called to do, we can know
that God is with us, and will give us what we need, even if
sometimes we need to ask for it in prayer.

January 27

[Moses said,] "It is the LORD who goes before you; he will be with you, he will not fail you or forsake you; do not fear or be dismayed."

DEUTERONOMY 31:8

At the end of his life, Moses handed off his role as prophet and leader of Israel to Joshua, reassuring him that God was with him; that God had called the Chosen People to the Promised Land; and that God's covenant meant that God was with them always. As we receive faith in God from the previous generation and hand it on to the next generation, we can have that same confidence: God is with us, and by covenant and Incarnation, has bound Himself to mankind forever.

January 28

The Lord commissioned Joshua, the son of Nun, and said, "Be strong and of good courage; for you shall bring the children of Israel into the land which I swore to give them: I will be with you."

DEUTERONOMY 31:23

God Himself confirmed the promises that Moses had made to Joshua; God called Joshua to be strong and steadfast because God Himself was with Joshua and the Israelites. God is good, and we are not; God is steadfast and true, even as we are not; and so we need not be afraid.

January 29

[The LORD said,] "Be strong and of good courage; for you shall cause this people to inherit the land which I swore to their fathers to give them."

JOSHUA 1:6

We who have been blessed with the Catholic faith, with Scripture, Tradition, and Magisterium; with the Sacraments, and devotions, and so much else — we have an obligation to be strong and steadfast by the grace of God in order to allow God to act in our lives and the lives of those around us. In order to love our neighbors rightly, we must first love God as He deserves — and then all things are possible.

January 30

[The LORD said,] "Only be strong and very courageous, being careful to do according to all the law which Moses my servant commanded you; turn not from it to the right hand or to the left, that you may have good success wherever you go."

JOSHUA 1:7

We are called to be children of God, which means to be holy as God is holy. That is only possible by God's grace, given to us through the Sacraments, especially Confession and the Eucharist. But if we remain close to Him, obeying His law, confessing our sins when we fail, and practicing a firm intent to do His will, we will see success beyond what we naturally would expect.

January 31

**[The Lord said,] "Have I not commanded you?
Be strong and of good courage; be not frightened,
neither be dismayed; for the Lord your God is with
you wherever you go."**
Joshua 1:9

The Book of Joshua, read in the spiritual sense, tells of the triumph of true religion over idolatry and infidelity in the soul. We can hear God's words to Joshua here as words to us, as a promise that if we hold on to God, He will ultimately vindicate us against the world, the flesh, and the devil.

FEBRUARY

February 1

The LORD said to Joshua, "Do not fear or be dismayed; take all the fighting men with you, and arise, go up to Ai; see, I have given into your hand the king of Ai, and his people, his city, and his land."

JOSHUA 8:1

All things become possible for those who have conformed their will to God's will. Remember the wisdom of Abraham Lincoln: "Sir, my concern is not whether God is on our side; my greatest concern is to be on God's side, for God is always right."

February 2

The LORD said to Joshua, "Do not fear them, for I have given them into your hands; there shall not a man of them stand before you."
JOSHUA 10:8

If God calls us to complete a task, He will also make it possible for us to do so. Sometimes we are called to be faithful rather than successful, to paraphrase St. Teresa of Calcutta, but when we are called to be successful, God will make a way.

February 3

Joshua said to them, "Do not be afraid or dismayed; be strong and of good courage; for thus the LORD will do to all your enemies against whom you fight."
JOSHUA 10:25

The Israelites could be confident in victory because they were obeying a call from God to go to the Promised Land and claim it. When we faithfully follow our vocational call, we can be confident that God's own strength acts on our behalf, and we will see wonders.

February 4

The LORD said to Joshua, "Do not be afraid of them, for tomorrow at this time I will give over all of them, slain, to Israel; you shall hamstring their horses, and burn their chariots with fire."

JOSHUA 11:6

The Book of Joshua is written as a story of national triumph. The message we should take away is that when Israel is faithful to God's call where to go and whom to fight, God leads the people to ultimate victory over all enemies, no matter how imposing.

February 5

The LORD turned to [Gideon] and said, "Go in this might of yours and deliver Israel from the hand of Midian; do not I send you?"

JUDGES 6:14

This is the summons from the Lord to Gideon, through whom God would achieve miraculous victories over the enemies of the Chosen People. He is a model of a faithful believer, answering a seemingly impossible call from God, and so witnessing God give him the victory.

February 6

The LORD said to [Gideon], "Peace be to you; do not fear, you shall not die."
JUDGES 6:23

Realizing he'd been speaking with a messenger of the Lord, Gideon feared the consequences. One of the essential lessons of the Bible is that only holy people may safely come before the ultimately holy. Jesus came to make holy us fallen sinners, and to draw us into right relationship with God. Jesus, our Savior, reassures us, "You are safe. Do not fear. You shall not die."

February 7

The LORD said to Gideon, "The people with you are too many for me to give the Midianites into their hand, lest Israel vaunt themselves against me, saying, 'My own hand has delivered me.'"
JUDGES 7:2

Sometimes, as we answer His call to a vocation or duty, God will allow us to be deprived of ordinary necessities in order to provide for us Himself in an extraordinary way. When times seem darkest, it's important to cry out to God. He is mighty to save; He loves us.

February 8

[Boaz said,] "Now, my daughter, do not fear, I will do for you all that you ask, for all my fellow townsmen know that you are a woman of worth."

RUTH 3:11

The widow Ruth, a Moabite, loved and trusted her Israelite mother-in-law, Naomi, whose advice led her to marry Boaz, a man of property. Through grief, loss, and living as a stranger in a strange land, Ruth's steadfast virtue allowed a happy conclusion to a terrible series of tragedies. Let us follow her example.

February 9

Then Samuel said to all the house of Israel, "If you are returning to the LORD with all your heart, then put away the foreign gods and the Ashtaroth from among you, and direct your heart to the LORD, and serve him only; and he will deliver you out of the hand of the Philistines."

I SAMUEL 7:3

Freedom from fear depends on freedom from idolatry — that is, not mistaking creatures for the Creator. God is almighty by nature; nothing else on earth or in Heaven is almighty by nature. By grace, we may share in the strength of God through the Sacraments and His generosity. So what have we to fear?

February 10

[Samuel said,] "But you have this day rejected your God, who saves you from all your calamities and distresses; and you have said, 'No! but set a king over us.' Now therefore present yourselves before the Lord by your tribes and by your thousands."

1 Samuel 10:19

So long as God was King over Israel, the Israelites had an incorruptible, perfectly wise, perfectly just, utterly trustworthy monarch. But they also had a monarch who couldn't be swayed by earthly power, money, or pleasure. How often do we prefer to listen to people who make us comfortable, who share our weaknesses or sins, rather than people who are in the right?

February 11

Samuel said to the people, "Fear not; you have done all this evil, yet do not turn aside from following the LORD, but serve the LORD with all your heart."

1 SAMUEL 12:20

Samuel called upon the Lord, and the Lord sent rain and thunder to indicate how evil the people had been. Yet Samuel reassured them, showing us that the right response to our own sinfulness isn't despair, but rather faithful service to the Lord. Our God does not desire our destruction, but rather seeks our salvation, so do not be afraid.

February 12

Saul said to Samuel, "I have sinned; for I have transgressed the commandment of the LORD and your words, because I feared the people and obeyed their voice."

1 SAMUEL 15:24

Fear of the Lord is the beginning of wisdom because it helps us keep our priorities straight. Don't do evil out of fear of the world, the power of your enemies, or the threats of hell. None of that has any strength in comparison to the might of God.

February 13

David said, "The Lord who delivered me from the paw of the lion and from the paw of the bear, will deliver me from the hand of this Philistine." And Saul said to David, "Go, and the Lord be with you!"

1 Samuel 17:37

David was a man after God's own heart, a man of trust, a man of passion, and a man of courage. He was willing to face the lion and the bear for the sake of his sheep, just as he was willing to face Goliath for the sake of his people Israel — just as his Lord and descendant, Jesus, the Son of David, would face suffering, death, and hell to save the lost sheep of Israel and all mankind.

February 14

[David said,] "All this assembly may know that the LORD saves not with sword and spear; for the battle is the LORD's and he will give you into our hand."
1 SAMUEL 17:47

When we are told to not be afraid, we're not simply being asked for self-control or gritted teeth. We can face the worst this life has to offer without fear, because we know our God is greater. By grace, we shall put our trust, not in the wisdom of the world, but in Jesus, the Word of God Incarnate.

February 15

[David said,] "Behold, as your life was precious this day in my sight, so may my life be precious in the sight of the LORD, and may he deliver me out of all tribulation."
1 SAMUEL 26:24

David would not lay a hand on Saul, the king, anointed by the prophet Samuel at the command of God. His hope for mercy as a result foreshadows the teaching of his greatest descendant, Jesus: "[T]he measure with which you measure will be measured out to you" (Mt 7:2)

February 16

David was greatly distressed; for the people spoke of stoning him, because all the people were bitter in soul; each for his sons and daughters. But David strengthened himself in the LORD his God.

1 SAMUEL 30:6

In a military catastrophe, David and his army were too late to save their wives and children from being taken captive by the enemy. In this moment of peril when David faced the prospect of a mutiny, he didn't put his trust in himself or any portion of the army; he put his trust in God. In the face of earthly catastrophe, we can and should do the same.

February 17

[Joab said,] "Be of good courage, and let us play the man for our people, and for the cities of our God; and may the LORD do what seems good to him."

2 SAMUEL 10:12

Good advice for an army before a battle; good advice for Christians setting to work on sharing the Gospel with our neighbors. Courage is contagious, as is cowardice, so it's important to set to work cheerfully, prayerfully, in obedience to God. He'll take it from there.

February 18

[David said,] "My God, my rock, in whom I take refuge, / my shield and the horn of my salvation, my stronghold and my refuge, / my savior, you save me from violence."
2 SAMUEL 22:3

David sang praise to God after he'd been delivered from his enemies. God gives us existence, sustains us, and saves us with His love and mercy; the least we can do (and the best!) is to give Him back thanks and praise!

February 19

[David said, "The LORD] reached from on high, he took me, he drew me out of many waters."
2 SAMUEL 22:17

Just as God had brought the created world out of the primordial chaos and nothingness; just as He had saved Noah and his ark from floodwaters; just as God saved the Israelites by parting the Red Sea, so had God saved David from the "deep waters" of his enemies. God acted with power for our forebears in the faith; He can act with power for us, today.

February 20

[David said, "The Lord] delivered me from my strong enemy,/ from those who hated me; / for they were too mighty for me. / They came upon me in the day of my calamity, / but the Lord was my stay."

2 Samuel 22:18-19

On our own, we are easily overwhelmed by the world, the flesh, and the devil. Even with friends, wealth, power, health, or other earthly goods, we can easily be overwhelmed by disaster. But God can draw good out of any evil. He is almighty, and the only one almighty by nature, willing to share His own strength with us by grace, so trust Him and do not be afraid.

February 21

[David said,] "You deliver a humble people,/ but your eyes are upon the haughty to bring them down."
2 SAMUEL 22:28

Beware the fairy tale of the self-made man! There's not a human being on the earth today who didn't depend on other human beings when we came into existence, and there's not a one of us who could exist independently of God, Creator and Sustainer. Humility, solidarity, and hospitality are realism; haughtiness, radical individualism, and pride are self-deception.

February 22

[David said,] "Yes, by you I can crush a troop, / and by my God I can leap over a wall. / This God – his way in perfect; / the promise of the LORD proves true; / he is a shield for all those who take refuge in him."
2 SAMUEL 22:30-31

David knew firsthand that if God wills it, we can do the impossible, the miraculous. If God gives the gift, all things are possible. Be men and women after David's own heart, which is after God's own heart, and trust in God before all others.

February 23

[David said,] "For you girded me with strength for the battle; /you made my assailants sink under me."
2 SAMUEL 22:40

As we witness in conflict after conflict, alliances matter in wartime. If God is your ally, who can overcome you?

February 24

Then David said to Gad, "I am in great distress; let us fall into the hand of the LORD, for his mercy is great; but let me not fall into the hand of man."
2 SAMUEL 24:14

David the King was wiser than his people, who had asked for an earthly ruler! Better to be in God's hands than the hands of any earthly power, for mercy is God's greatest attribute, and indeed, one of His names. The same can't be said for the world, the flesh, or the devil.

February 25

Elijah said to [the widow], "Fear not; go and do as you have said; but first make me a little cake and bring it to me, and afterward make for yourself and your son."
1 KINGS 17:13

Elijah the prophet had asked a poor widow, a stranger and foreigner, for food, even though she had barely enough for one last meal for her and her son. He called her to trust in him and his God. When she did so, miracles ensued.

February 26

The angel of the LORD said to Elijah, "Go down with him; do not be afraid of him." So he arose and went down with him to the king.
2 KINGS 1:15

The wicked king had sent messages calling Elijah a "man of God," even though the king persisted in fighting against the prophet. But Elijah truly was a prophet of the Lord, and so the Lord vindicated him. If we walk the path God lays before our feet, we have nothing to fear, even if that path leads to the Cross.

February 27

[Elisha said,] "Fear not, for those who are with us are more than those who are with them."
2 KINGS 6:16

It's one of the greatest passages about angels in the entire Bible: When the king of Aram sends an army against the prophet Elisha, the servant of the prophet is scared. But Elisha sees the reality of the situation, and prays for his servant's eyes to be opened to see the hosts of Heaven surrounding them. If we are men and women of God today, the angels will be there for us, too!

February 28

"You shall not fear other gods, but you shall fear the LORD your God, and he will deliver you out the hand of all your enemies."
2 KINGS 17:39

Idolatry, or giving creatures the worship due to God, traps us in fear because it traps us in lies. It's false, unreal, attributing power to powerless things. Right worship will set us free from fear because we won't expect from creatures what we will never receive from them. God, the Creator and Sustainer of everything, can give us whatever we need.

February 29

Isaiah said to them, "Say to your master, 'Thus says the LORD: Do not be afraid because of the words you have heard, with which the servants of the king of Assyria have reviled me.'"

2 KINGS 19:6

In response to lying words from the Assyrians, claiming that Israel's God would not or could not rescue His people, the prophet Isaiah summoned the Israelites to courage. Given the grace and might of God, we need not be afraid even of the sins and wickedness of others. God's mercy and justice are more powerful.

MARCH

March 1

**Jabez called on the God of Israel, saying,
"Oh, that you would bless me and enlarge my border, and
that your hand might be with me, and that you would
keep me from harm so that it might not hurt me!"
And God granted what he asked.**

1 CHRONICLES 4:10

We are to pray with confidence in the love and generosity
of God, expecting all good things from Him. That doesn't
mean we'll always get what we pray for as we specified it,
just as children don't always get what they want from their
father. But God will answer our prayers, and that answer
will come from His wisdom, His power, and His mercy.

March 2

When they received help against them, the Hagrites and all who were with them were given into their hands, for they cried to God in the battle, and he granted their entreaty because they trusted in him.

1 CHRONICLES 5:20

Jesus, I trust in You! **"The graces of My mercy are drawn by means of one vessel only, and that is — trust. The more a soul trusts, the more it will receive"** (*Diary of Saint Maria Faustina Kowalska*, 1578). We may not receive the answer we expect or want when we pray, but with perfect trust will come graces beyond imagining.

March 3

[Joab said,] "Be of good courage, and let us play the man for our people, and for the cities of our God; and may the LORD do what seems good to him."
1 CHRONICLES 19:13

Even when we're faithful to prayer, the Sacraments, works of mercy, and obeying the will of God as given through Scripture, Tradition, and the Magisterium, sometimes, we may be overcome on earth by our enemies (the world, the flesh, or the devil). That's when we need the wisdom of Jo'ab. We must do what is right, and if God wills that we go to Calvary with His Son, may God be praised!

March 4

[David said to his son, Solomon,]
"You will prosper if you are careful to observe the
statutes and ordinances which the LORD commanded
Moses for Israel. Be strong, and of good courage.
Fear not; be not dismayed."

1 CHRONICLES 22:13

David was a prophet as well as a king, and here he warns
his son Solomon of the sins that would destroy him. True
strength, true fearlessness, comes from loving, trusting
obedience of God. Prayer is so important because in any
relationship, good communication is essential. Further,
we can't obey God's laws on our own strength. We need
the grace that comes through prayer.

March 5

[David said to his son, Solomon,] "Take heed now, for the LORD has chosen you to build a house for the sanctuary; be strong, and do it."

1 CHRONICLES 28:10

David had planned to build a Temple for the Lord, a place to house the Ark of the Covenant and allow for the worship of God. But God reserved that task to Solomon, David's son. Similarly, another Son of David, Jesus, "builds" the new Temple: Himself, Body, Blood, Soul, and Divinity. Through Jesus, we may bring everything to God the Father in prayer, praise, and thanksgiving.

March 6

Then David said to Solomon his son, "Be strong and of good courage, and do it. Fear not, be not dismayed; for the Lord God, even my God, is with you. He will not fail you or forsake you, until all the work for the service of the house of the Lord is finished."

I Chronicles 28:20

"Courage" is essentially to have or take "cor," which is Latin for "heart." So David, a man after God's own heart, is exhorting his son to take heart. Set aside fear of the future or of the task before you; take heart and invite the Holy Spirit into yourself and your situation. Doing God's work means God will be with you, and His purposes achieved (even if those purposes are not what we expect).

March 7

[Solomon said,] "Whatever prayer, whatever supplication is made by any man or by all your people Israel, each knowing his own affliction, and his own sorrow and stretching out his hands toward this house; then hear thou from heaven your dwelling place, and forgive, and render to each whose heart you know, according to all his ways (for you, you only, know the hearts of the children of men)."

2 CHRONICLES 6:29-30

Solomon begged God to make the newly-built Temple a true house of prayer for the Chosen People of God. In a similar way should every parish church, every place where the Blessed Sacrament is reserved in the tabernacle, be a focus for our prayer. Jesus is with us wherever we are, but He is present in a special way in the Eucharist. We know where to find God in the flesh, even now, for all that the world has forgotten.

March 8

[The Lord said to Solomon,]
"If my people who are called by my name humble
themselves, and pray and seek my face, and turn from
their wicked ways, then I will hear from heaven, and
will forgive their sin and heal their land."

2 Chronicles 7:14

According to St. Augustine, throughout Scripture, the goal is to return to the sort of close communion with God that we had before the fall, when God breathed life into Adam and Eve, and they saw God face-to-face. When Jesus came, that goal was achieved, and mankind again saw the face of God. Look at the Divine Mercy Image, bring all your blessings and burdens, and speak face-to-face with Jesus, the face of the Father's Mercy.

March 9

**When the LORD saw that they humbled themselves,
the word of the LORD came to Shemaiah: "They have
humbled themselves; I will not destroy them, but I will
grant them some deliverance, and my wrath shall not be
poured out upon Jerusalem by the hand of Shishak."**

2 CHRONICLES 12:7

In humility is sanctity and safety. In humility, we are made
pure. Pride invites destruction, but humility opens the door
for God to be God and for us to be His creatures, His beloved
children. Have you sinned? Humble yourself before God, and
all will be well. Have you done good things? Humble yourself
before God, and all will be well.

March 10

**Asa cried to the LORD his God,
"O LORD, there is none like you to help, between the
mighty and the weak. Help us, O LORD our God,
for we rely on you, and in your name we have come
against this multitude. O LORD, you are our God;
let not man prevail against you."**

2 CHRONICLES 14:11

The weaker we are, the more confident we may be in the
help of the Lord. "I did not come to call the righteous
but sinners" (Mk 2:17). The worse the chances of
victory, the greater the confidence we should have in the
help of the Lord, even if that help doesn't look like what
we expect or want.

March 11

[Azariah said,] "When in their distress they [Israel] turned to the LORD, the God of Israel, and sought him, he was found by them."

2 CHRONICLES 15:4

The modern world is convinced that God is silent, inaccessible, far off, and His existence is unprovable, His miracles a distant memory. Practicing Catholics should know this is not true. Jesus waits for us in every tabernacle across the world; God speaks in the Scriptures; miracles continue to this day; everything speaks of God. Seek the Lord, and you will find Him.

March 12

[Azariah said,] "But you, take courage! Do not let your hands be weak, for your work shall be rewarded."

2 CHRONICLES 15:7

If we follow the way of the Lord, even though it lead through the valley of the shadow of death, we shall find unexpected assistance along the way. If we set to the task before us and persevere to the end, the graces and the fruits will be beyond imagining.

March 13

**[Hanani the seer said to Asa, king of Judah,]
"Were not the Ethiopians and the Libyans a huge
army with exceedingly many chariots and horsemen?
Yet because you relied on the LORD, he gave them
into your hand."**

2 CHRONICLES 16:8

True prophets don't always tell the future, but they do
always tell the truth. Hanani the seer rebukes Asa, the king
of Judah, reminding him of how the Lord had brought
great victories in the past. But because Asa had relied on
a neighboring king rather than on God, Asa would now
have to face a number of wars. The issue isn't meeting
problems with reasonable solutions, but rather trusting
earthly means more than we trust in God.

March 14

[King Jehoshaphat said,] "O our God, will you not execute judgment upon them? For we are powerless against this great multitude that is coming against us. We do not know what to do, but our eyes are upon you."
2 CHRONICLES 20:12

Jehoshaphat begins with wisdom; he begins with prayer. God is mighty to save, but He often waits on the invitation of His people to intervene. Have you invited the intervention of the Lord in the hard situations facing you right now? Have you welcomed His Will, whatever it may be? We don't always get a clear, obvious answer, but opening the door to God's action is more important than we can imagine.

March 15

[Jahaziel said,] "Listen, all Judah and inhabitants of Jerusalem, and King Jehoshaphat: Thus says the Lord to you, 'Fear not, and be not dismayed at this great multitude; for the battle is not yours but God's.'"

2 Chronicles 20:15

Fear not. There's a mighty army coming against you, but fear not. God's got this, so fear not. That's such a hard thing to do, and yet if we actually listen to the promise and the One making it, what a great joy! God will sort out the evil confronting us; He will find a way through it for us. All we have to do is trust, watch, wait, and pray.

March 16

[Jahaziel said,] "You will not need to fight in this battle; take your position, stand still, and see the victory of the LORD on your behalf, O Judah and Jerusalem. Fear not, and be not dismayed; tomorrow go out against them, and the LORD will be with you."
2 CHRONICLES 20:17

Sometimes, we are handed battles to fight. But sometimes, we are told by God to stand down. Obeying in trust may be harder than fighting, for who wants to have to face onrushing power and evil with a peaceful heart, standing quietly, waiting on the Lord? Yet here, that's exactly what God said to do. He called on His people to go out in opposition to the enemy, but also to wait for God's own intervention. A summons to trust, indeed!

March 17

[King Hezekiah said,] "Be strong and of good courage. Do not be afraid or dismayed before the king of Assyria and all the horde that is with him; for there is one greater with us than with him."

2 CHRONICLES 32:7

Many Christians have given way to fear of the enemies of Christ and His Church; Scripture rebukes us and reminds us that God is greater than any earthly power. Even the lords of the mightiest earthly empires in their moment of victory may be routed by God's intervention, or through the quiet, seemingly insignificant efforts of God's little ones.

March 18

So the LORD saved Hezekiah and the inhabitants of Jerusalem from the hand of Sennacherib king of Assyria and from the hand of all his enemies; and he gave them rest on every side.
2 CHRONICLES 32:22

The path of the Lord is the path of peace, and of rest. God is mighty to save, and can make use of any evil or suffering to allow grace into the world, if only we unite our sufferings to the Cross of Christ. God is greater than any earthly power, even the mightiest of empires, and so even when evil seems to have the upper hand, we can persist in hope.

March 19

When [King Manasseh] was in distress he entreated the favor of the LORD his God and humbled himself greatly before the God of his fathers.

2 CHRONICLES 33:12

Why does God permit suffering? All too often, it's the only way to save us from ourselves. Great Christian spiritual writers have noted again and again how blind we can be during times of prosperity. God must often allow our idols (money, power, pleasure, etc.) to fail us before we will turn to Him, the true God, once again.

March 20

[Nehemiah] looked, and arose, and said to the nobles and to the officials and to the rest of the people, "Do not be afraid of them. Remember the LORD, who is great and terrible, and fight for your brethren, your sons, your daughters, your wives, and your homes."

NEHEMIAH 4:14

Fear of the Lord is the beginning of wisdom in large part because it reduces our fear of everything and everyone else. God who is Good is the Almighty, not worldly powers, authorities, or even the devil with all of hell. Next to God, they are as nothing. Remember the Lord, who is great and terrible, and live the words "Jesus, I trust in You!"

March 21

"For they all wanted to frighten us, thinking, 'Their hands will drop from the work, and it will not be done.' But now, O God, strengthen my hands."
NEHEMIAH 6:9

If we work for God in His holy city, the Church, and are obedient to the call of God, we will face trials from the world, the flesh, and the devil. When that happens, we must turn to prayer, like Nehemiah, and beg God to strengthen our hands.

March 22

And the LORD said to Satan, "Have you considered my servant Job, that there is none like him on the earth, a blameless and upright man, who fears God and turns away from evil? He still holds fast his integrity, although you moved me against him, to destroy him without cause."

JOB 2:3

Here in the Old Testament, in the story of Job, we see one of the clearest foreshadowings of the sufferings of Jesus: a righteous man, more so than anyone else on earth, with integrity intact. The mystery of the sufferings of Job is answered by the mystery of the Incarnation and the sufferings of Jesus. Bad things happen to good people, and it will be made right by the Son of God who joins the good in their suffering, and who will, in His Justice and Mercy, make all right in the end.

March 23

[Job] said to [his wife], "You speak as one of the foolish women would speak. Shall we receive good at the hand of God, and shall we not receive evil?" In all this Job did not sin with his lips.

JOB 2:10

Here we see Job's heroic virtue, and his realism. We've received so much good — our lives; our families. We don't wonder why we've received so much good. Why should we wonder when we receive evil? And yet, as we shall see, Job certainly cried out to God for answers. Here is wisdom: Complain to God, but do not complain about God.

March 24

"Why is light given to him that is in misery, / and life to the bitter in soul...?"

JOB 3:20

How many times across the centuries have people suffering terrible evil echoed the cry of Job? How many of us can recognize this: Why am I still alive when those whom I love are dead? Why am I well when my beloved is suffering? Our hope is in the Resurrection and the world to come.

March 25

**"My friends scorn me; /
my eye pours out tears to God…"**
JOB 16:20

Even in the times of the Old Testament, righteousness looked like Jesus: innocent, falsely accused of sin, and suffering in a mysterious way. God ultimately vindicates Job and Jesus; so, too, can we hope that, in the end, "He will wipe every tear from their eyes, and there shall be no more death or mourning, wailing or pain, [for] the old order has passed away" (Rev 21:4).

March 26

**"But he knows the way that I take; /
when he has tried me, I shall come forth as gold."**
JOB 23:10

Jesus told us to be like Job — that is, to be wise as serpents and innocent as doves (see Mt 10:16). If we suffer, it should be in spite of our innocence, our goodness; we should suffer like the saints, offering up everything in union with Jesus' sacrifice "in atonement for our sins and those of the whole world."

March 27

[The Lord said,] "Shall a faultfinder contend with the Almighty? / He who argues with God, let him answer it."
Job 40:2

The ultimate faultfinder isn't the Just Judge; rather, it's the devil, the accuser of the brethren (see Rev 12:10). We are welcome to cry out to God in our distress; we are welcome to bring every wound and suffering to God; we are welcome to wonder why bad things happen to good people — but all this must arise from our trust in the goodness, power, and love of God, not faultfinding.

March 28

**"Who is this that hides counsel without knowledge?' /
Therefore I have uttered what I did not understand, /
things too wonderful for me, which I did not know."**
JOB 42:3

The answer to Job's sufferings and questions is God
Himself, God face-to-face with Job. Think of how the
presence of a parent or a spouse is such a consolation
during times of suffering. Later in the book, God says that
Job had spoken well of Him — that Job's baffled love and
trust of God were true, while the excuses offered by Job's
friends merit a curse. Evil and suffering are true mysteries;
their answer is equally mysterious: Jesus on the Cross
and rising from the grave.

March 29

"He is like a tree / planted by streams of water, / that yields its fruit in its season, / and its leaf does not wither. / In all that he does, he prospers."

PSALM 1:3

King David, tradition tells us, also wrote many of the Psalms, making his prayer the model for Jews and Christians alike. David was a man after God's own heart (see Acts 13:22); praying the Psalms is a way of training our hearts to also be like God's, like the Sacred Heart of the Son of David, of Jesus. The more like Jesus we are, the more true this passage will be of us: We will be like trees planted by streams of water and yield plentiful, good fruit.

March 30

[David said,] "I am not afraid of ten thousands of people / who have set themselves against me round about."

PSALM 3:6

If God is with us, numbers don't matter. The Lord, the Creator and Sustainer of everyone and everything, is mightier than all, so be sure to stand with God so that He might stand with you.

March 31

[David said,] "Answer me when I call, O God of my right! / You have given me room when I was in distress. / Be gracious to me, and hear my prayer."

PSALM 4:1

There are times where we feel alone and are tempted to be very afraid. God doesn't simply tell us to not be afraid. Rather, Scripture tells us and shows us that we need to cry out to God; we need to trust His love, knowledge, and power enough to ask Him for the help we need, rather than simply being upset that times are so hard. The great commandments are about love, and love needs trusting communication.

APRIL

April 1

[David said,] The LORD is a stronghold for the oppressed, / a stronghold in times of trouble.

PSALM 9:9

Be with the Lord in good times so that He will be with you in bad times. Remain with God and no matter what comes, you may have confidence in the grace of God to bear the burdens or transform them into blessings.

April 2

[David said,] "In the LORD I take refuge; / how can you say to me, / 'Flee like a bird to the mountains?'"

PSALM 11:1

If God calls us to retreat, then go with God we must. But if God has called us to stand, even in the face of overwhelming odds, then the wisest course of action is to stand and face the oncoming tide. Our safety is in the will of the Lord. As Jesus said, "For whoever wishes to save his life will lose it, but whoever loses his life for my sake will find it" (Mt 16:25).

April 3

"Because the poor are despoiled, because the needy groan, / I will now arise," says the LORD; "I will place him in the safety for which he longs."
PSALM 12:5

A good life tip: Be someone whose name the poor bless. Make sure you are performing one or more of the works of mercy regularly. If you are spoken of favorably by the poor, the Lord will hear and bless you. If, on the other hand, you oppress the poor, we are warned in Matthew 25 what might be the result.

April 4

[David said,] "I keep the LORD always before me; / because he is at my right hand, I shall not be moved. / Therefore my heart is glad, and my soul rejoices; / my body also dwells secure."
PSALM 16:8-9

If God is with us, we are in the best of company. Or rather, if we are with God, we have chosen the safest possible place, the best possible side, the one stable ground on which to stand. True security is betting on the Lord of Life, the eternal One, the God of all.

April 5

[David said,] "He reached from on high, he took me, / he drew me out of many waters."
<small>PSALM 18:16</small>

As God saved Noah from the flood, so too can He save us from the daily deluge of worries and cares. God is greater than our problems, our pride, or our sorrow. God is mighty to save, even if that salvation looks like a wounded Man bearing the Cross alongside us.

April 6

[David said,] They came upon me in the day of my calamity; / but the LORD was my stay. / He brought me forth into a broad place; / he delivered me, because he delighted in me.
<small>PSALM 18:18-19</small>

Even our worst days can become days of victory if we abide in trust in the Lord. Let the Light of the Word into your darkest days, and He will shine all the brighter for you and through you to the rest of the world. God is mighty to save, and so we need to let Him into the situations where we most need saving.

April 7

**[David said,] "Yes, by you I can crush a troop; /
and by my God I can leap over a wall."**
PSALM 18:29

"For man this is impossible, but for God all things are
possible" (Mt 19:26). By God, we can do the miraculous.
We can be merciful as our Father in Heaven is merciful
(see Lk 6:36). We can forgive our enemies and do good to
those who persecute us, praying even for those who
do evil, as Jesus commanded (see Lk 6:27-35).

April 8

**[David said,] For thou didst gird me with strength for the
battle; / thou didst make my assailants sink under me.**
PSALM 18:39

In this valley of tears, we will suffer and face opposition.
Let us stand with the Lord. Let us say to God, "Thy will
be done." Then we shall set ourselves on the winning
side, for God is the almighty, capable of bringing a greater
good even out of the greatest evil. Look to the Cross!
Where we seem defeated, there we have won.

April 9

For the king [David] trusts in the LORD; / and through the steadfast love of the Most High he shall not be moved.
PSALM 21:7

All earthly authorities are at their best when they remember they are not the ultimate authorities. Rather, all authority comes from God, who permits kings to rule. But all earthly powers pass, and all worldly fortunes eventually crumble. Only through steadfast love does an eternal royal lineage, the Davidic kingdom, exist, for Jesus, the Son of David, is King.

April 10

For he [the LORD] has not despised or abhorred / the affliction of the afflicted; / and he has not hid his face from him [David], / but has heard, when he cried to him.
PSALM 22:24

God isn't merely the God of the powerful, the proud, or the healthy. God doesn't turn His face away from the afflicted, the despised, the suffering soul. No! He came to seek out those farthest from Him. Jesus, sent to the sinners, said to St. Faustina, **"The greater the sinner, the greater the right he has to My mercy"** (*Diary*, 723).

April 11

[David said,] "Even though I walk through the valley of the shadow of death, / I fear no evil; / for you are with me; / your rod and your staff, / they comfort me."
PSALM 23:4

Jesus is the Good Shepherd, the Son of the David who composed these words. Jesus has already walked through worse than the valley of the shadow of death. He has gone into death itself, and triumphed.

April 12

[David said,] "My eyes are ever toward the LORD, / for he will pluck my feet out of the net."
PSALM 25:15

What a powerful image! Imagine a hunting dog caught in a net, waiting on its master, looking with eagerness and trust toward him. That's David, waiting on the Lord. He knows God is all powerful and trustworthy, and so he looks to God even in the midst of a trap. God is our hope, even when all seems hopeless.

April 13

**[David said,] "The LORD is my light and my salvation; /
whom shall I fear? / The LORD is the stronghold
of my life; / of whom shall I be afraid?"**

PSALM 27:1

Earthly strength can break and fail. Worldly wealth can run out,
be stolen, or simply be insufficient. Pleasure depends on health
and appetite. Pride depends on us not noticing that we are
creatures, not the Creator. Everything else will fail us if we try
to take it apart from God, but if we rest in God, we rest secure.

April 14

**[David said,] "Though a host encamp against me, /
my heart shall not fear; / though war arise against me,
yet I will be confident."**

PSALM 27:3

The worst thing to ever happen has already happened. God
died on a Cross one Friday afternoon long ago. Everything
before that and everything after is but a shadow of that
tragedy. Nothing worse can ever happen, thank God, so
even if we see evils rise and enemies ring us about, we can
be confident. God came out of the grave; we will never face
something worse.

April 15

[David said,] "Wait for the LORD; / be strong, and let your heart take courage; / yes, wait for the LORD!"
PSALM 27:14

This definitely isn't the advice of modern-day leaders to their people today: "Be strong; have courage … and wait!" We are told to act and never leave a problem unsolved. Is this possible? Not if the problem is too big for our finite abilities. God is God, and we are not. So in the face of some crosses, we ought to wait on the Lord.

April 16

[David said,] "Incline your ear to me, / rescue me speedily! / Be a rock of refuge for me, / a strong fortress to save me!"
PSALM 31:2

What a prayer! How often do we feel exactly like this? Scripture shows us that praying for divine help and deliverance is a constant in the life of the children of God. And the witness of prophets like King David shows us that these prayers are answered — at times in mysterious ways, yes, and in God's time, not according to our schedule, but powerfully answered, nonetheless.

April 17

[David said,] "I had said in my alarm, / 'I am driven far from your sight.' / But you heard my supplications, / when I cried to you for help."

PSALM 31:22

Even if we have fallen; even if it feels like we can't see God, or His power and presence in the created world, or hear His voice — even if we are driven far from God's sight, He can hear us and will come to our aid.

April 18

[David said,] "Be strong, and let your heart take courage, / all you who wait for the LORD!"

PSALM 31:24

During dark times, waiting on the Lord can seem a foolish choice, an impossible or imprudent gamble. Yet God is utterly trustworthy, as Jesus proved in the Incarnation and proves through the lives of the saints. Jesus is the surest bet we could ever make, so be strong and let your heart take courage. We who choose to believe in Jesus shall not be put to shame for our faith.

April 19

**[David said,] "Our soul waits for the LORD; /
he is our help and shield."**
PSALM 33:20

Waiting on the Lord sounds very passive, and yet it's more
like tenants waiting on the landlord's arrival, or employees
awaiting the arrival of the owner of the company, or children
awaiting their parents' return home. That is to say, if we wait
on the Lord effectively, we'll have prayed, confessed, fasted,
and done a lot to prepare!

April 20

**[David said,] "I sought the LORD, and he answered me, /
and delivered me from all my fears."**
PSALM 34:4

Faith is a journey, with Jesus as its beginning, for without
Him nothing was made. Faith has Jesus as its destination, for
He is the goal of all creation. And faith is a pilgrimage with
Jesus as our companion on the way, for we could not come to
Him without His help. We are lost sheep. We must be carried
home by the Good Shepherd, by the Good Samaritan.

April 21

[David said,] "This poor man cried, and the LORD heard him, / and saved him out of all his troubles."
PSALM 34:6

God has given the rich many good things already; the poor may cry to God with confidence, for God Himself lived on earth as a poor man with nowhere to lay His head (see Mt 8:20). He knew hunger. He knew thirst (see Jn 19:28). Jesus knows the needs of the poor, and will answer the prayers of the poor. Let us all seek to be part of that answer, and faithfully perform the works of mercy.

April 22

[David said,] "When the righteous cry for help, the LORD hears, / and delivers them out of all their troubles."
PSALM 34:17

We ask the saints for their prayers because they are the truly righteous, and powerful are their prayers! But we also turn to God with trust, even when we have sinned, knowing that He loves us. Indeed, He sent His only-begotten Son to save us from our sins (see Rom 5:10). Cry to God with trust, invoking Jesus' name, and wait for wonders.

April 23

**[David said,] "Many are the afflictions of the righteous; /
but the LORD delivers him out of them all."**
PSALM 34:19

The Scriptures don't preach to us some "prosperity
Gospel" message of perfect comfort and earthly success
if we follow the Law of God. No — Scripture is realistic,
sharing the Jewish and Christian experience of relationship
with God. We may hope for ultimate victory, but here
in this valley of tears, many are the afflictions of the
righteous. Face them with God, and be at peace.

April 24

**[David said,] "Do not fret because of the wicked, /
be not envious of wrongdoers!"**
PSALM 37:1

Here is wisdom, and also hard, hard teaching. How can
we see the wicked prosper in the world and not wonder
what happened to the justice of God? And yet that's
exactly the summons here. Bring every concern to God
in prayer, and then be at peace, ready to respond to
God's call or to simply wait on the Lord.

April 25

[David said,] "Be still before the LORD, and wait patiently for him; / do not fret over him who prospers in his way, / over the man who carries out evil devices!"
PSALM 37:7

Christian courage, fearlessness, comes with trust in God, and trust in God demands waiting on the Lord, ready to act when He calls, patiently resting when He doesn't, and bringing all troubles to prayer so that we may abide in peace.

April 26

[David said,] "The LORD helps them and delivers them; / he delivers them from the wicked, and saves them, / because they take refuge in him."
PSALM 37:40

Jesus sheds new light on this passage through His ministry. The righteous are saved by God because they take refuge in Him — that is, the righteous are made righteous by God. We only have any claim to righteousness by the grace of God freely offered to us through the Word of the Lord and through the Sacraments.

April 27

[David said,] "He [the Lord] drew me up from the desolate pit, / out of the miry bog, / and set my feet upon a rock, / making my steps secure."

Psalm 40:2

Jesus established a Church on the Rock, on Peter (see Mt 16:18). He drew us up out of the bog, out of the mire of error and sin, and through Scripture and Sacred Tradition, especially as defined by the Magisterium, gives us the Deposit of Faith. Go to Confession and Mass. Study Scripture and the *Catechism of the Catholic Church*. Pray and perform works of mercy.

April 28

[David said,] "As for me, I am poor and needy; / but the Lord takes thought for me. / You are my help and my deliverer; / do not delay, O my God!"
PSALM 40:17

David speaks for all of us here. We are, as a whole, strangers in a strange land, poor and needy compared to God's plan for us to be adopted sons and daughters in an unfallen world. We were created for paradise, for the Garden of Eden, not the present fallen world. In truth, the whole human race can pray for deliverance from this present darkness. Jesus is our hope; Jesus, I trust in You!

April 29

Why are you cast down, O my soul, / and why are you disquieted within me? / Hope in God; for I shall again praise him, / my help and my God.

PSALM 42:11

God is with us at our lowest, and with us at our highest. He is eternally steadfast, a rock for all ages, since without Him, nothing exists at all. So we may be assured that He has not abandoned us, even when times are hardest, for if He had abandoned us, we would have ceased to exist. Each breath is an "I love you" from God.

April 30

... for not by their own sword did they win the land, / nor did their own arm give them victory; / but your right hand, and your arm, / and the light of your countenance; / for you delighted in them.

PSALM 44:3

Facing impossible challenges? Bring to bear the infinite might of God by asking His guidance and support. He may summon us to repentance, challenge us to set aside our earthly treasures, and walk a path we'd never have chosen for ourselves, but He will overcome everything for our good.

MAY

May 1

God is our refuge and strength, / a very present help in trouble. / Therefore we will not fear though the earth should change, / though the mountains shake in the heart of the sea...
PSALM 46:1-2

God is our stability in the midst of a world in the grip of titanic change, of times and seasons that seem more like waves on the sea than ordinary history. God is unchanging Goodness, Beauty, and Truth, on whom we can found our lives and to whom we can always reach out, no matter where we are.

May 2

There is a river whose streams make glad the city of God; / God is in the midst of her, she shall not be moved; / God will help her when morning dawns.

PSALM 46:5-6

We are promised that through living the faith and receiving the Sacraments, streams of living water shall flow from within us (see Jn 7:38). We are made the temples of the Holy Spirit (see 1 Cor 6:19). We are the city of God, each of us individually in the state of grace and all of us together in the Mystical Body of Christ. By the grace of God, we, like Christ our Head, can say, "Destroy this temple and in three days I will raise it up" (see Jn 2:19), for Jesus, Divine Mercy Incarnate, is the Resurrection and the Life (see Jn 11:25).

May 3

**[God said,] "… call upon me on the day of trouble; /
I will deliver you, and you shall glorify me."**
PSALM 50:15

Many of the Psalms are as much about reminding the singer
and the audience to trust in God as they are about praising
God and His promises. We often forget to call on God in
times of trouble. We get so stressed or are in so much pain
that all we can do is put one foot in front of the other. But
even if it's hard, we need to be choosing to include God
in our hard times. We need to remember to eat, to sleep,
to drink, and to pray. We may feel numb; we may not feel
faithful. But talk to God regardless.

May 4

[David said,] "But I call upon God; / and the Lord will save me. / Evening and morning and at noon / I utter my complaint and moan, / and he will hear my voice."

PSALM 55:16-17

Why do prayers seemingly go unanswered? Sometimes, the answer is that we aren't persisting in prayer (see Lk 18:1-8). Look to the example of St. Monica, who cried out to God with tears for the salvation of her son. Eventually, he did convert, and went on to become the great Bishop Augustine of Hippo, a Doctor of the Church, and a father of Christian civilization. All this, because she did not set down the burden of prayer. She did not stop, even after years of apparently unanswered prayers.

May 5

**[David said,] "Cast your burden on the LORD, /
and he will sustain you; / he will never permit /
the righteous to be moved."**

PSALM 55:22

David is a realist. Everything already rests on God. Without
God, we would cease to exist. God is both Creator and
Sustainer. Creation was not a one-and-done action; rather, it
continues from moment-to-moment as God holds everything
in existence with remembrance and love. So He's already
holding all of us and our burdens in existence. Why don't you
set down the mental and emotional weight, as well? Why not
acknowledge reality and let God give you a hand with that
cross? He's all loving and all powerful, a Father mighty to
save. Give Him the things that are weighing you down.

May 6

[David said,] "When I am afraid, / I put my trust in thee. / In God, whose word I praise, / in God I trust without fear. / What can flesh do to me?"

PSALM 56:3-4

"The beginning of wisdom is fear of the Lord, / and knowledge of the Holy One is understanding" (Prov 9:10). The essential thing it teaches is that there is nothing in the created world worth fearing. God alone is God; He is ultimate power; He is greatness. So of what should we be afraid? It's the sort of truth of the faith that can be incredibly demanding (there are plenty of threatening people or things in this world), but also incredibly liberating (God is more fearsome than all of them, and guess what? He loves us absolutely!). "If God is for us, who can be against us?" (Rom 8:31).

May 7

**[David said,] "In God I trust without fear. /
What can man do to me?"**
PSALM 56:11

The Psalms make better sense when you put them in the
context of David's life. These aren't the words of a man for
whom everything always went his way. David faced the wrath
of a mad king and the betrayal of his own son. He had his
nose rubbed in his own sinfulness and its consequences. He
fought wars. He won and lost. He succeeded and he failed.
Throughout it all, he returned again and again to trust in the
Lord, to call out to God. He knew that even as the day-to-day
struggles and difficulties take place, ultimately, God will have
His way. So what can man do to us?

May 8

[David said], "Be merciful to me, O God, be merciful to me, / for in you my soul takes refuge; / in the shadow of your wings I will take refuge, / till the storms of destruction pass by."

PSALM 57:1

We live in times plagued by great storms, both natural and preternatural, both weather-related and political, or religious, or economic, or … the list goes on. But now is the time of mercy, as Jesus told St. Faustina. Now is the time to turn to the Divine Mercy, to appeal to it for ourselves and our loved ones, for our friends and our enemies. Now is the time to take shelter with the Holy Family, in the arms of the Good Shepherd, beneath the mantle of the Immaculate Mother of God, and under the protection of the cloak of St. Joseph.

May 9

**[David said,] "But I will sing of your might; /
I will sing aloud of your steadfast love in the morning. /
For you have been to me a fortress /
and a refuge in the day of my distress."**
PSALM 59:16

It's important to be grateful to God for all He is doing and all He has done. After all, the central act of worship of our Catholic faith is the Eucharist, which means "thanksgiving." All that we are comes from God; all that we may yet be comes from God. Our past is a gift from God, our present is a gift from God; our future is a gift from God. So let us sing of His might! Let us sing aloud of His steadfast love in the morning! God has been very good to us. Sing of it! It will be light and encouragement for you and others.

May 10

**[David said], "With God we shall do valiantly; /
it is he who will tread down our foes."**

PSALM 60:12

"For man this is impossible, but for God all things are
possible" (Mt 19:26). David's promise of victory here is
echoed by the Son of David, by Jesus, the Divine Mercy
Incarnate, when He spoke to St. Faustina about the Divine
Mercy Image. **"I promise that the soul that will venerate
this image will not perish. I also promise victory over
[its] enemies already here on earth, especially at the
hour of death. I Myself will defend it as My own glory"**
(*Diary*, 47, 48). Bring God into your struggles; venerate
Jesus in the Divine Mercy Image with trust.

May 11

[David said,] " … from the end of the earth I call to you, / when my heart is faint. / Lead me to the rock that is higher than I; / for you are my refuge, / a strong tower against the enemy."

PSALM 61:2-3

The king is crying out from his sickbed to God for assistance here. How often have we all cried out to God when we were sick, even during minor illnesses? The Church has always known that care of the sick was part of her mission, especially in light of the many miracles of healing worked by Jesus during His life on earth. We rightly turn to God, the source of all life and strength, asking for His assistance. But Christ reveals to us the true reach of God's love and power. He not only can give health; He can share His own divine life with us.

May 12

**[David said,] "Trust in him at all times, O people; /
pour out your heart before him; / God is a refuge for us."**
PSALM 62:8

Here is the spirituality of the Divine Mercy message and
devotion. Trust in God at all times, the good, the bad,
and the ugly. Trust in God, and we will find in Him a
refuge. Sometimes, He will make our troubles go away.
Sometimes, He will give us the strength to bear them.
Sometimes, He will give us a glimpse of the larger plan,
of the graces and consequences of our fidelity. And sometimes, He will simply keep us company in the dark night.
Always, He is with us. Always, He loves us.

May 13

**[David said], " … for [God] has been my help, /
and in the shadow of your wings I sing for joy. /
My soul clings to you; / your right hand upholds me.**
Psalm 63:7-8

To be overshadowed by God is to be incredibly blessed. It is to be a temple of the Holy Spirit, a gate of Heaven and a house of God, like our Blessed Mother. How can we keep from singing for joy? God has been our help from the first moment of our existence, and if we've been walking with the Lord for any length of time, it's almost certain we have memories of special graces, particular times when we felt His presence or witnessed His power at work. Remember, and give Him thanks and praise!

May 14

[David said,] "By dread deeds you answer us with deliverance, / O God of our salvation, / who are the hope of all the ends of the earth, / and of the farthest seas ... "
PSALM 65:5

Our God is an awesome God, something we can take for granted or else treat as a simple slogan. But the power of God in action is a dreadful thing, even when it works for the good. Fear of the Lord is the beginning of wisdom, because even as He is supreme Love, He is also supreme Power. Our God is great beyond words, great beyond our comprehension. He is our hope, and He is our shield. We may approach Him with trust and love because of the Paschal Mystery, because of Jesus Christ, because of God's covenants with us all. But let us not forget the mystery and majesty of divinity.

May 15

[David said,] "Blessed be the LORD, / who daily bears us up; / God is our salvation."
PSALM 68:19

Without God, we would be nothing. God, "I am who am" created us all from nothing, and without God who is Being itself, nothing would exist. He sustains us in existence from moment to moment, daily bearing us up. And more: As we try to walk the Christian path, we are helped by grace. On our own, we would fall into sin and never get out again. With God, we may rise again and again on the way home to Him. "For man this is impossible, but with God all things are possible" (Mt 19:26).

May 16

[David said,] "[God] who made me see many sore troubles / will revive me again; / from the depths of the earth / you will bring me up again."
PSALM 71:20

King David was a true prophet, and foretold throughout the psalms the coming of Christ the Lord. Here, he foretells the general resurrection without perhaps realizing all that he is saying. The ultimate Christian answer to evil and suffering is that this life is not all there is; death is not the end; there will be a general judgment, and a resurrection of every person who has ever lived. God who sustains us in life will bring us back from death. Be not afraid! "Death is swallowed up in victory. / Where, O death, is your victory? / Where, O death, is your sting?" (1 Cor 15:54-55).

May 17

[Asaph said,] "In the day of my trouble I seek the LORD; / in the night my hand is stretched out without wearying; / my soul refuses to be comforted."

PSALM 77:2

Here is trust. Here is love of God. Here is belief in God's goodness, His love, and His power. God doesn't ask us to suffer silently, alone. He doesn't ask that we "tough it out." He wants us to come crying to Him in our times of distress. "Blessed are they who mourn, / for they will be comforted" (Mt 5:4). Refusing to beg God for help is a symptom of the pride of the devil. We must all learn to accept charity, as well as to give it, if we are to be saved and enter Heaven.

May 18

He [God] led them in safety, so that they were not afraid; / but the sea overwhelmed their enemies.

PSALM 78:53

Faith for the Israelites was about believing, remembering, and transmitting the memories of God's signs and wonders to their ancestors. God had proven Himself again and again; the Israelites had plenty of reason to believe in Him and place their trust in Him. When times are hard, it can be difficult to remember happier times or reasons for hope. Remember the saints and wonders of the past, even in darkest days.

May 19

**In distress you called, and I [God] delivered you; /
I answered you in the secret place of thunder; /
I tested you at the waters of Meribah.**
PSALM 81:7

The Psalms are written in the context of the enormous acts of
God that marked Israel's past. In distress, Israel cried out to
God from their place of slavery in Egypt, and God delivered
them with signs and wonders on a scale rarely seen in all of
salvation history. On Mount Sinai, God spoke to the people,
but the people were so afraid, they sent Moses alone in their
stead. God was faithful even when the people rebelled, feeding
them and taking care of them throughout the entire journey
in the wilderness.

May 20

[David said,] "In the day of my trouble I call on you, / for you do answer me."
PSALM 86:7

David here says the same thing a later, greater Son of David will say: "Ask and it will be given to you; seek and you will find; knock and the door will be opened to you" (Mt 7:7). We are assured in Scripture that God hears every prayer, and that God answers every prayer. But we are also told persistence is necessary (see Lk 18:1-8), and we see from our own experience that the answer at times can be, "Not now" or "Not like that." Our prayers are not magic, but love letters to God the Father in Heaven. We are family members, and we speak like loving family.

May 21

He [God] will cover you with his pinions, / and under his wings you will find refuge; / his faithfulness is a shield and buckler. / You will not fear the terror of the night, / nor the arrow that flies by day...

PSALM 91:4-5

As chicks find protection under the wings of their mother, so too do we find protection under the wings of the Lord, under the sheltering protection of His love and mercy. No matter what dangers we face, God is there with us, beside us. No matter what evils we suffer, God is there with us. He took on Himself all sin, and underwent death. There is no evil that has not been made a potential means of grace through the self-sacrifice and the sufferings of Jesus.

No matter what, He is with us.

May 22

Because he cleaves to me in love, I [God] will deliver him; / I will protect him, because he knows my name. / When he calls to me, I will answer him; / I will be with him in trouble, / I will rescue him and honor him.

PSALM 91:14-15

Divine protection doesn't come because we find just the right words, or just the right gestures, or just the right way to compel God to do what we want. No. God summons us to faith, trust, and love. God calls on us to be like Him, who is Love and Mercy. If we love God and neighbor, we will be delivered from evil: suffering in this life, but looking forward to Heaven and the Resurrection. We will be as Lazarus, beloved by God, who can even rescue us from death.

May 23

**When the cares of my heart are many, /
[God's] consolations cheer my soul.**
PSALM 94:19

When your mind is pinging around; when the to-do
list seems eternal; when the demands on your time are
endless, welcome God in. The saints have noted that
people of prayer seem at peace in the heart of the storm,
and at times, seem to have endless amounts of time. There
are consequences to opening time up to eternity, after
all, and we do that at Mass, in prayer, and when we turn
to God with trust and love in our ordinary working lives.
Change your day. Let it be a day of the Lord.

May 24

**Do not hide your [God's] face from me /
in the day of my distress! / Incline your ear to me; /
answer me speedily in the day when I call!**
PSALM 102:2

Christians know that God's face is now a human face, and it's always turned toward us. Indeed, Jesus awaits us in every tabernacle in every Catholic church around the world. God's face is not now nor ever will be hidden from us, if only we turn to Him in the Sacraments, in the Church. He is there for us, waiting for us to turn to Him, to come to Him again when He calls with mercy and grace.

May 25

Many times [God] delivered them, / but they were rebellious in their purposes, / and were brought low through their iniquity. / Nevertheless he regarded their distress, / when he heard their cry.

PSALM 106:43-44

This is perhaps the single most hopeful truth taught us by Scripture: Sin is not the final word. Our failures, our falls do not forever and eternally break off our communion with God so long as we turn to Him again and again with trust. Ask God for forgiveness! He wants to help you. Ask God for the grace to do better, even if doing better means you come to Him more quickly the next time you fall. God loves us, even when we are stuck in sinful habits, whether that be anger, or gluttony, or drink, or drugs, or sex, or greed. "If we are unfaithful / he remains faithful, / for he cannot deny himself" (2 Tim 2:13).

May 26

**Then they cried to the LORD in their trouble, /
and he delivered them from their distress ...**
PSALM 107:28

Scripture shows us that grumbling about God leads to further
problems down the line, but grumbling to God brings grace,
change, and wonders. Why? If we don't think someone cares
about our problems or believes he lacks the power to do
anything about them, we grumble about him. If, on the other
hand, we know someone is wise, powerful, and loves us dearly,
then we go to them in our troubles, knowing that we will
find everything from a sympathetic ear to a solution to our
problems. Trust God. Turn to Him.

May 27

**Then they were glad because they had quiet, /
and he [God] brought them to their desired haven.**
PSALM 107:30

For some of us, it's all too easy to get bored with quiet, to
wish that our lives were a little more adventurous. Peace
and quiet can sometimes feel more like a burden rather than
a blessing. But for far too many nations around the world,
peace and quiet, a gentle and ordered life, is a distant dream.
Let us not forget the immense blessing of peace, of quiet, of
order. Let's seek our adventure by following God, by obeying
Scripture, Tradition, and the Magisterium, and so preserve our
hearts in peace and quiet.

May 28

**[David said,] "With God we shall do valiantly; /
it is he who will tread down our foes."**
Psalm 108:13

Find where God stands and stick by Him. If we go to Him,
we shall ultimately find ourselves on the winning side. Now,
that doesn't look like what our earthly expectations may lead
us to believe. Look at the stories in Scripture! Following God
may lead to persecution, exile, or any number of difficulties.
But it will also lead to signs and wonders, to a pillar of fire by
night and a pillar of cloud by day leading us to the Promised
Land (see Ex 13:21). It will make us like Jesus, and the
Crucifixion was followed by the Resurrection.

May 29

He is not afraid of evil tidings; /
his heart is firm, trusting in the LORD.
PSALM 112:7

Imagine being able to watch the news with peace in your
heart! Imagine confronting the incredible dangers of the
modern world with serenity. That is what comes from
trust in the Lord, from the spirituality of Divine Mercy,
from a Christian heart in the state of grace abiding with
the love and mercy of God. But being at peace doesn't
mean ceasing to love God and neighbor, ceasing to speak
truth or do works of mercy. No — peace frees us to serve
God and our neighbor. It liberates us from the exhaustion
of despair.

May 30

For [God] has delivered my soul from death, / my eyes from tears, / my feet from stumbling...
PSALM 116:8

For David, this is autobiographical. God really had saved him from death in the most literal fashion on a number of occasions. God had spared him mourning; God had set his feet on straight paths. God had done all this for David, and David knew that God would do it for the rest of His beloved children, as well. That didn't mean David never mourned, or never stumbled; it did mean that God was always there for him, always loving, always true. Trust in the Lord more than you trust in yourself, or in earthly things.

May 31

**Out of my distress I called on the LORD; /
the LORD answered me and set me free.**
PSALM 118:5

There are certainly times in our lives where we call on
the Lord and He seems to remain silent. But there are
also many times where we are in trouble and we don't
call on the Lord. We may not want to bother Him with
something we think is too small for His concern, or we
may have a sneaking suspicion that no one, not even God,
can help us out. Set aside all fear, doubt, or trepidation.
Prayer is always answered, but not always at the speed or
in the manner we expect. What matters most in prayer is
our persistence, our trust, and our love.

JUNE

June 1

**With the LORD on my side I do not fear. /
What can man do to me?**
PSALM 118:6

If we stand with God, then God will be with us, and
we shall have nothing to fear. God gives us clear signs
through Scripture, Tradition, and the Magisterium
of where He may be found, and where His side is.
Follow those signposts; taken all together, they will
not lead you astray.

June 2

"This is my comfort in my affliction / that your promise gives me life."
PSALM 119:50

In deepest darkness, in starkest tragedy, still we may stand on the earth knowing that God is God and we are not; that the end of the world is marked by the return of Jesus and the final defeat of the devil; that we shall see the resurrection of the dead. The promise of God has come with a down payment: the miracles of Jesus and His saints; the endurance of the Church in spite of every form of corruption or opposition; the fulfilled prophecies; and the beauty, truth, and works of mercy spread in the world through members of the Church. The promise of God is sure, even when all else seems to have failed us.

June 3

**"Trouble and anguish have come upon me, /
but thy commandments are my delight."**
PSALM 119:143

The Law of the Lord set out for the faithful Israelite a safe
road, mapping the will of God for His Chosen People. For
the faithful Christian, we know that that road, that Law,
both has been fulfilled and that the Law of God has a
name and a face: Jesus Christ, the Divine Mercy Incarnate.
Because of Jesus, we know that God's justice is His mercy,
that His law is love, and that His commandments are life.
We know that God is our Father first and foremost, by the
grace of the Incarnation. We know that in all the trouble
and anguish of this present darkness, the Light shines and
is not quenched. Good has the final word, not evil.

June 4

"Princes persecute me without cause, / but my heart stands in awe of your words."
PSALM 119:161

Scripture keeps hammering away at the difference between the worldly power that we all too often mistake for real strength, real might, and the true power of God (see, for instance, Ps 146:3-5). After all, we can watch the government do things! We can see armies on the march, watch weapons be fired and bombs explode. That's power — right? It's a far more limited power than it seems, and God's power is far greater than we notice. After all, God is sustaining the entirety of creation, past, present, and future, from moment to moment. The Word of God has a greater power than the mightiest earthly prince.

June 5

"I lift up my eyes to the hills. / From where does my help come? / My help comes from the Lord, / who made heaven and earth."

Psalm 121:1-2

What other help is like the help of God? Who could compare to the might and power of God? "If God is for us, who can be against us?" (Rom 8:31). And yet God's ways are not our ways, and His victories do not always look like the sort of victory we wanted. His help may be the strength needed to endure persecution, martyrdom, and death, after all. Our triumph may be like the triumph of the martyrs. Our faith is a help and support for the reality of life in this world, not the lies of the so-called prosperity Gospel or the notion that positive thinking can overcome all evils. No! Our sign is the Cross, and our victory is the empty tomb.

June 6

**Those who trust in the LORD are like Mount Zion, /
which cannot be moved, but abides for ever.**
PSALM 125:1

What a promise for those of us devoted to the Divine Mercy!
Here is the fruit of the spirituality summarized by "Jesus, I
trust in You." Trust in the Lord leads to stability, constancy,
and is a path to overcoming the world, the flesh, and the
devil. Think of saints like Joan of Arc or the Apostles. In the
eyes of the world, they had no power, no preparation for the
tasks Heaven would set them. After all, what could a peasant
girl do to the armies of England? What could fishermen, a tax
collector, and a handful of ordinary Judeans do in the face
of persecution by Rome? And yet the saints are remembered
forever, mighty to intercede for us from Heaven, and the
power and memory of the mighty who opposed them fades.

June 7

"It is in vain that you rise up early / and go late to rest, / eating the bread of anxious toil; / for he gives to his beloved sleep."
PSALM 127:2

This verse corrects the workaholics among us, as well as those of us who remain awake out of worry or avoidance of the next day. God blesses us with the gift of rest, even going so far as to command it. Indeed, one of the characteristics of the righteous throughout the Old and New Testaments is the ability to rest. Consider St. Joseph, a righteous man (see Mt 1:19), hearing from an angel in his dreams (see Mt 1:20-21; 2:13; 2:19-20; 2:22). Consider Jesus, asleep in the boat during the storm (see Mk 4:38-40). So get good sleep, and get enough of it. Ask God to prosper the work of your hands so that you can sleep the sleep of the just.

June 8

"Sorely have they afflicted me from my youth," let Israel now say, "… yet they have not prevailed against me."
PSALM 129:1-2

The grace of God doesn't always end persecution or worldly suffering. Instead, it strengthens us and prepares us to face what comes. If we abide in prayer, living life in the Spirit and doing our best to remain in a state of grace, we will have the assistance of God's limitless strength throughout our lives. That doesn't mean we shall never break or fail; after all, we are fallen human beings, lacking the original gifts God had intended for us. But God has equipped us in the Sacraments and His many providential gifts to get back up, to abide, to endure. Let us continue to practice our faith, to study the treasures of Divine Revelation in Scripture, Tradition, and the Magisterium, so as to be equipped for all righteousness (see 2 Tim 3:17).

June 9

**[David said,] "I have calmed and quieted my soul, /
like a child quieted at its mother's breast; /
like a child that is quieted is my soul."**
PSALM 131:2

This short Psalm is a celebration of what happens when
a faithful soul allows God to be God, and surrenders any
attempt at all knowledge or all control. We are creatures;
God is the Creator. We are limited; He is infinite. That allows
us to be at peace, for the greatest problems of the world are
not up to us to solve. If God wanted, every person would
be converted in an instant, and every mouth fed, and every
problem solved. And yet God permits and sustains the world
as it is. Why? We can get a glimpse of an answer in free will
allowing for the existence of true love, but even then, there's
mystery in the ways of the world. That's all right. Do your bit,
love God and neighbor, and be at peace. God is in control.

June 10

**[David said,] "On the day I called, you answered me, /
my strength of soul you increased."**
PSALM 138:3

God's answer to our prayers often isn't to heal the physical
illness or bring an earthly fix to a difficult situation. Often,
God gives us the grace to endure, the virtue we need in order
to carry our crosses. It often doesn't feel like a very generous
or helpful answer. After all, confronted with intolerable
tragedy, I'd rather have the tragedy fixed than I would the
strength to tolerate it. But God intends us to be His children,
and God bears us and our sins with incredible patience, even
to the point of enduring the Passion. Our model, then,
is Jesus. That's why we walk the Stations of the Cross and
pray the Sorrowful Mysteries of the Rosary.

June 11

**[David said,] "Search me, O God, and know my heart! /
Try me and know my thoughts!"**

PSALM 139:23

David is wise. God sees all and knows all anyway. There
is nothing hidden from the omniscience of God. So why
bother to hide anything from Him? Instead, come to God
in all honesty, acknowledging your sins as well as your
sacrifices, your weaknesses as well as your strengths. God
sees you, knows you, loves you, not the face you put on
for the world. Branding is meaningless in Heaven. All
that matters is what's true, what's real. God knows us as
we are, and can heal the wounds we actually have. He is
Light, which shines through all illusions and chases away
any darkness. Be honest with Him now and let Him chase
away your darkness. Welcome His healing grace.

June 12

**[David said,] "I cry with my voice to the LORD, /
with my voice I make supplication to the LORD, /
I pour out my complaint before him, /
I tell my trouble before him."**

PSALM 142:1-2

Here, David models prayer for us. Jesus said to St. Faustina, **"Daughter, give Me your misery, because it is your exclusive property"** (*Diary*, 1318). We are not meant to suffer alone, to endure by our own strength and muscle our way through life. No! Instead, we are meant to live life as a conversation with God. For the saint, every deed and word is part of that relationship, the giving and receiving of life and love, the endless dance of persons, Creator and creature, in a self-giving and endlessly receptive relationship. In other words, God gives us everything, and we are meant to give everything back to God. That includes our needs, our wants, our concerns. Prayer is definitely thanks and praise. It's also petition and lament.

June 13

[David said,] "For your name's sake, O LORD, preserve my life! / In your righteousness bring me out of trouble!"
PSALM 143:11

"Save Your reputation, God! Vindicate me, a believer, in the eyes of the world, for my vindication is Your vindication!" It's a bold prayer, one that depends on us having been blameless before God. It's the sort of prayer best prayed after going to Confession and receiving Holy Communion in the state of grace. But it's still a prayer worth praying. Why? Because we are created in order to know and love God. If God's name is sullied in the sight of the nations, then it becomes all the harder for them to come to know and love Him. Woe to us if God's name is sullied because of our actions! Blessed are we, though, if we turn to God with love and trust in the midst of our misfortunes. We act with wisdom!

June 14

[David said,] "The Lord is near to all who call upon him, / to all who call upon him in truth. / He fulfils the desire of all who fear him, / he also hears their cry, and saves them. / The Lord preserves all who love him; / but all the wicked he will destroy."

PSALM 145:18-20

In the lives of Jesus and the saints, we see the extraordinary breadth of this promise as well as its limits. We see in signs and wonders, in miracles and impossible things, that the desire of those who fear the Lord will be answered even when those desires are impossible. We see resurrections and healings. But we also see the agony of Jesus in the Garden of Gethsemane, the Cross at Calvary, and the tomb in stone. We see that the preservation of the righteous doesn't always look like the sort of comfort and worldly security we'd want by nature.

June 15

[God said,] "He who listens to me will dwell secure / and will be at ease, without dread of evil."
PROVERBS 1:33

This teaching only makes sense in light of the joy and fear-lessness of the martyrs. So many have gone to their deaths proclaiming Jesus with supernatural courage, supernatural confidence. Indeed, the Spirit of God makes possible all virtue, and all good. What does it mean that we shall have no dread of evil? It means that evil will have over us only the same power it had over Jesus. We may suffer for a time and even die, but we will rise again. We will triumph, even from beyond the grave. A Christian life, in order to be a virtuous life, must be characterized by trust in God, not by fear of the world, the flesh, or the devil.

June 16

[Solomon said,] "Trust in the Lord with all your heart, / and do not rely on your own insight."

PROVERBS 3:5

We may be mistaken, but the Lord will not be mistaken. We may be driven by unruly or disordered passions (Solomon proved that!), but God will not be so driven. We are given intellect and will, and told to use them, but we must also know that they have limits. Even the wisest man can be wrong, and the greatest of the angels became the devil himself. Trust in the Lord, and He will be light in even the darkest of nights. Do not rely on your own insight, but rather repose with the Truth Himself.

June 17

[Solomon said,] "If you sit down, you will not be afraid; / when you lie down, your sleep will be sweet."
PROVERBS 3:24

Solomon is promising the rewards of a life founded on fear of the Lord; that is, on trust in God, His power, His justice, and His mercy. This is a life characterized by seeking wisdom and living according to its precepts. With wisdom comes work, certainly, and many burdens, but it also means that you are faithful to God, relying on Him. If you remain with God, then God will have your back. You will be able to be vulnerable in this world as Jesus was vulnerable, and not be afraid, as the martyrs have proven; you will be able to lie down and rest easy. You will even be able to follow the Lord to the threshold of death and be joyful as you cross, for He has gone before us even there, and returned.

June 18

[Solomon said,] "The righteous is delivered from trouble, / and the wicked gets into it instead. / With his mouth the godless man would destroy his neighbor, / but by knowledge the righteous are delivered."

PROVERBS 11:8-9

Wisdom and virtue can deliver us from many evils. A virtuous life can make many challenges much easier! Anyone who's gone camping knows that proper planning and preparation can make all the difference in the world to how comfortable and fun the experience is. At the same time, Christ and His Cross show the limit of all such promises of the blessings of righteousness. Sometimes, the godless do destroy the righteous. Sometimes, the gossips win. But Calvary and similar experiences in our lives don't change the fact that this proverb offers much wisdom. Truth wins; real quality, real virtue survives the test of time and of the bad opinions of those around us.

June 19

[Solomon said,] "Anxiety in a man's heart weighs him down, / but a good word makes him glad."
<small>PROVERBS 12:25</small>

All Christians are called to carry our crosses in obedience to and imitation of Jesus, our teacher, our master, and our friend (see Mt 16:24-26). And St. Paul assures us that we will not be tested beyond our strength (see 1 Cor 10:13).

However, if we choose anxiety over trust, we can take the crosses God has allowed for us and make them way beyond our strength. We can weigh ourselves down!

June 20

[Solomon said,] "When a man's ways please the LORD, / he makes even his enemies to be at peace with him."
PROVERBS 16:7

Here is a true gift! The method outlined in Romans 12:20 shows us how Christian living can make enemies into friends. Indeed, this proverb resembles the promise our LORD gave to St. Faustina about the Divine Mercy Image: **"I promise that the soul that will venerate this image will not perish. I also promise victory over [its] enemies already here on earth, especially at the hour of death. I Myself will defend it as My own glory"** (*Diary*, 47, 48). And yet, of course, our LORD's own life shows us that victory over our enemies can look like Calvary. True victory, Christian victory, doesn't guarantee we will never face suffering or persecution in this life.

June 21

[Solomon said,] "The fear of the Lord leads to life; / and he who has it rests satisfied; / he will not be visited by harm."

PROVERBS 19:23

Fear of the Lord means we recognize where real power, real wealth, real wisdom can be found. All good things come from God; He, therefore, is a greater good than any created good thing. God's love for us is better than pleasure, worldly security, earthly power, or any wealth. God's favor is more worth having than any skill, any mastery or attainment in any field. Nothing is worth the price of our soul. Nothing is more valuable than our relationship with God. Fear of the Lord casts everything else into the shade. If we have God, we have Life. If we have Life, of what can we be afraid? If we are alive in the Spirit, even death need no longer be fearsome.

June 22

**[Solomon said,] "Fret not yourself because of evildoers, /
and be not envious of the wicked."**
PROVERBS 24:19

It can be incredibly tempting to look at the wealth, power,
talent, or achievement of people who have stopped at
nothing to reach the top in this world. Indeed, we live in
a culture geared to encouraging that sort of envy in us.
Look at the latest fashions! Don't you want to look like
these models? Look at the wealthy! Don't you want to live
like them? Look at the powerful! Don't you want to be
like them? But Scripture summons us, not just to refuse to
imitate the wicked, but even to surrender our envy of their
worldly attainments. Our whole hearts need to be converted
by grace. We need to love God more than we love His gifts.

June 23

**[Solomon said,] "The fear of man lays a snare, /
but he who trusts in the LORD is safe."**
PROVERBS 29:25

How often do we do stupid things out of fear? How often do
we stress about things that never happen, or make anxious
plans to deal with problems that never arise? Don't get me
wrong. Prudent preparation and planning is wise. But fear
often leads to bad decisions. Trust in God, on the other hand,
is the parent of prudence, temperance, justice, and fortitude,
as well as faith, hope, and love. Trust in God, the Just Judge
and the Divine Mercy, leaves us room to be merciful and
forgiving to others. We can ask God for the strength we need
to meet the evils of each day, and for the assistance to behave
like His children, no matter what cross may come.

June 24

[Solomon said,] "Strength and dignity are [a good wife's] clothing, / and she laughs at the time to come."
PROVERBS 31:25

A wise woman isn't afraid of worldly evils, even the most powerful. A wise woman is a woman of faith, a woman who knows that fear of anything other than God isn't allowed to a child of the covenant, to a descendant (spiritual or physical) of the Israelites whom God set free from slavery in Egypt, whom He rescued by unheard-of miracles, whom He sustained for 40 years in the wilderness, and 40 more after that. A child of God has nothing to fear in this world, no matter how big or scary evil may seem. We are in the hands of God; we are summoned to a spirituality of trust. Jesus, I trust in You!

June 25

[The Preacher said,] "What has a man from all the toil and strain with which he toils beneath the sun?"
ECCLESIASTES 2:22

Ecclesiastes is a grim book in many ways, but sometimes the very best wisdom comes by building on the base of the worst case scenario. The exhausted, world-weary tone of much of the book suggests a writer who has seen too much, and so is uniquely well-qualified to write about how all the idols of life aren't enough. Pleasure? He's seen and done pleasure. Power? He knows power. Wealth? No substitute for the Almighty. The author has grown weary of this world, suggesting by his very weariness that we are not made for this fallen present age. Instead, "Our help is in the name of the Lord, / who made heaven and earth" (Ps 124:8).

June 26

[The Preacher said,] "For everything there is a season,
and a time for every matter under heaven: /
... a time to weep, and a time to laugh; /
a time to mourn, and a time to dance."
ECCLESIASTES 3:1,4

Are you burdened now with sorrow, difficulty, or tragedy?
This wintry season of suffering will pass, and it will be spring
again. Are you blessed now with joy, ease, or triumph? Enjoy
the harvest, for sorrow will come again. Saint Ignatius of
Loyola spoke of the times of consolation and desolation. He
also offered the wisdom that no major decisions should be
made in a time of desolation. Do not let fear govern you, for
its day comes and goes; rather, thank God for His blessings,
ask for help carrying the burdens, and no matter what, keep
the lines of communication open with Heaven.

June 27

[The Preacher said,] "Remove vexation from your mind, and put away pain from your body; for youth and the dawn of life are vanity."

ECCLESIASTES 11:10

When we are young, it is silly to borrow trouble, to look ahead to all the possible sorrows of life and to bear burdens before they arrive for us to bear. As many wise spiritual writers have said, we are blessed with the sacrament of the present moment, the closest we come to living in eternity like God. In the present moment, we are able to act. We can't change the past or guarantee the future. We can only choose now to be virtuous, to live according to prudence, to do the right thing, and to enjoy the blessings of life. Remember that even this fallen world is not wholly bad; indeed, much good remains. "For God so loved the world that he gave his only begotten Son" (Jn 3:16).

June 28

And the LORD said to Isaiah, "Go forth to meet Ahaz ... and say to him, 'Take heed, be quiet, do not fear, and do not let your heart be faint because of these two smoldering stumps of firebrands, at the fierce anger of Rezin and Syria and the son of Remaliah.'"

ISAIAH 7:3-4

There are "smoldering stumps of firebrands" all over our media landscape today, pouring forth an endless incitement to anger and fear in their audience. Christians are called by Scripture to a different path. Remember the fruits of the Holy Spirit: "love, joy, peace, patience, kindness, generosity, faithfulness, gentleness, self-control" (Gal 5:22-23). Worldly fear and panic stampede us and disrupt our life in the Spirit. We lose those gifts. Consider: Does the news I watch or the public figures whom I follow encourage in me worldly fear or the dispositions of the Spirit? Am I following worldly firebrands or people alive with the Holy Spirit?

June 29

[The Lord said,] "Do not call conspiracy all that this people call conspiracy, and do not fear what they fear, nor be in dread. But the Lord of hosts, him you shall regard as holy; let him be your fear, and let him be your dread."
ISAIAH 8:12-13

Our era is plagued by an endless proliferation of half-truths. You can find them in the news, on podcasts and chat forums, on endless social media platforms. Ultimately, we need to place our trust in Jesus. Men, even brilliant, powerful, and wealthy men, do not control history. God is the Lord of History. As Jesus told Pontius Pilate, "You would have no power over me if it had not been given to you from above" (Jn 19:11).

June 30

Thus says the LORD, the LORD of hosts: "O my people, who dwell in Zion, be not afraid of the Assyrians when they smite with the rod and lift up their staff against you as the Egyptians did."

ISAIAH 10:24

Scripture is against all anxiety. Again and again, the Israelites are told not to be afraid of anything. They are to fear the Lord, and Him alone. Indeed, there seems to be an implicit connection in the wisdom of Scripture between fearing a thing and making it into an idol. That means that fear, properly speaking, is reserved for God alone ... and ultimately, as we grow in a relationship with Him, learning to love and trust Him, that fear transforms and becomes simply an aversion out of love to ever offending Him. So in our modern world, so dedicated to constantly finding new things for us to fear, remember the wisdom of Scripture.

JULY

July 1

Behold, God is my salvation; / I will trust, and will not be afraid; / for the LORD God is my strength and my song, / and he has become my salvation.

ISAIAH 12:2

What a difference it makes when the Lord is our salvation rather than worldly power, wealth, strength, or wisdom! What a difference when our fate doesn't depend on anything so weak and unpredictable as our own selves! In our weakness is our strength, for when we know we are weak, when we know our strength is insufficient in the face of the demands a fallen world can make on us, that's when we turn to God and ask for His assistance. He is all-powerful, and so can bring to bear overwhelming force against any evil, any suffering, any darkness. When God is in our lives, how blessed are we!

July 2

**For you have been a stronghold to the poor, /
a stronghold to the needy in his distress, / a shelter
from the storm and a shade from the heat; /
for the blast of the ruthless is like a storm against a wall,
/ like heat in a dry place.**

ISAIAH 25:4-5

Scripture upends the logic of the world. We are used to assuming that if you want power, it's best to do good things for the powerful. If you want wealth, it's best to do favors for the wealthy. Better that the ruthless consider us their friends than their enemies! But God tells us through His prophets that if we want true security, true protection from evil, true assistance in our times of need, then we must be of assistance to the poor. It's no use serving the ruthless, the merciless; we ought to be servants, instead, of mercy, and those in need of mercy. Jesus takes this a step further: If we help the poor, we help Him personally (see Mt 25:31-46).

July 3

Open the gates, that the righteous nation which keeps faith may enter in. / You keep him in perfect peace, whose mind is stayed on you, because he trusts in you.
ISAIAH 26:2-3

One of the hardest tasks God ever sets for us is to be at peace. Why? Because our inner peace depends upon faith and believing in His promises. The Lord God proved to the Israelites His power and fidelity when He brought them out of Egypt, sustained them through their decades of wandering in the wilderness, and saw them to a kingdom in the Promised Land. The signs and wonders that accompanied His prophets from Moses on down remain some of the greatest in all of human history. And the gift of Jesus, the signs and wonders that accompanied His time on earth, and the graces given through the Church and the saints ... well, we've been given spectacular reasons for faith, hope, love, and peace.

July 4

**For thus said the LORD God, the Holy One of Israel, /
"In returning and rest you shall be saved; / in quietness
and in trust shall be your strength."**

ISAIAH 30:15

It's tempting to be big and loud, or to follow big and loud
people. After all, the squeaky wheel gets the grease, right?
But true strength is demonstrated in restraint, in mastery.
The expert fighter isn't the one who makes the biggest
bang, but the one who gets the biggest bang for his buck.
Our God is true; our faith is true; our Sacraments are real;
the Lord Jesus is in fact king of Heaven and earth. And
so we can rest; we can be quiet and trust. As the Gospel
shows time and again, worldly success isn't the measure
that matters. Worldly power and money pass away, or
corrupt those who covet them, and serve well those who
hold them lightly, generously. True strength is revealed in
quiet people who get things done, like St. Joseph.

July 5

Then justice will dwell in the wilderness, and righteousness abide in the fruitful field. / And the effect of righteousness will be peace, / and the result of righteousness, quietness and trust for ever.
ISAIAH 32:16-17

For a people suffering invasions, exile, and an uncertain present, the promise of quietness and trust is attractive. If we want quiet and trust, then we need to set to work in pursuit of a just society. The way is laid out in Catholic social teaching, especially as it's presented in the papal encyclicals on social issues and the *Compendium of Catholic Social Doctrine*. Then we won't need to fear bandits in the wild places or the destruction of our fertile fields and bustling cities. No! With justice and righteousness comes enough for all.

July 6

O LORD, be gracious to us; we wait for thee. / Be our arm every morning, / our salvation in the time of trouble.
ISAIAH 33:2

Waiting on the Lord can be incredibly hard, especially for those of us used to the principle if you see something wrong, you say something; if you see a problem, fix it. But sometimes, the best, most effective thing we can do is wait. If someone needs surgery, I shouldn't grab a knife and start cutting; that person needs a hospital and an expert surgeon, not a well-intentioned amateur. We all do the best we can in loving our neighbor, but sometimes, our neighbor needs the Divine Physician Himself. Sometimes, we may think that we need to solve other peoples' problems when, in reality, what's called for is the spiritual poverty of peace and waiting. When He acts, it will be perfectly, completely.

July 7

**Say to those who are of a fearful heart,
"Be strong, / fear not! / Behold, your God will come
with vengeance, with the recompense of God. /
He will come and save you."**

Isaiah 35:4

These are words that must be spoken with the grace of the
Holy Spirit behind them, or else they ring very hollow. But
saints and martyrs across the centuries have verified their truth.
The vengeance of the Lord in this time of mercy often doesn't
look like what we'd want. There isn't often instant retribution
for sins against us. In fact, in many cases, there's mercy and
forgiveness instead. But there's no more perfect response
to an enemy than making them into a friend, no more total
victory. "God proves his love for us in that while we were still
sinners Christ died for us" (Rom 5:8). Our salvation looks like
a happy death, a blessed stay in Heaven, and resurrection to
glory at the end of time. The Lord's vengeance, most perfectly
executed, looks like the Cross.

July 8

Isaiah said to them, "Say to your master, 'Thus says the Lord: Do not be afraid because of the words that you have heard, with which the servants of the king of Assyria have reviled me.'"

Isaiah 37:6

King Hezekiah feared for the welfare of his people when the servants of the King of Assyria had spoken ill of God. After all, when a pipsqueak insults a soldier in a bar, the rest of the patrons clear out! But God sent word through His prophet for the people to not be afraid, that He would send retribution upon the King of Assyria in the king's own land. When in doubt or fear, speak to the Lord God. Ask Him for what you need. Tell Him of your worries. Bring everything to Him. He knows all and can do all, but He also often waits to be asked. He has made us children, not machinery. He raises us as children; He doesn't manipulate us like a puppet master. He treats us like people. So be sure to ask, and listen for the answer in Scripture and the workings of Divine Providence!

July 9

Lo, it was for my welfare that I had great bitterness; / but you have held back my life from the pit of destruction, / for you have cast all my sins behind your back.
ISAIAH 38:17

At the end of his life, King Hezekiah offered a hymn of thanksgiving to God. Here, he gives testimony that, like anyone facing hard times, he had felt bitterness in the face of his many trials and tribulations. But Hezekiah is wise. He recognizes the goodness of God, the providential care that God had had for him, in spite of his sins. Indeed, God owes us nothing beyond what He has promised us. God gives us life, salvation, and every good thing; our sins merit destruction. But the Lord is generous and merciful. He blesses where He might legitimately condemn. He saves us from our own sins and from ourselves. He is the Good Shepherd, and all too often, we are very sinful, very silly sheep. Thank God for Divine Mercy!

July 10

[The LORD] gives power to the faint, and to him who has no might he increases strength.

ISAIAH 40:29

Of ourselves, we can do nothing. By nature, we are limited creatures. We tire easily; we must sleep every night, have days off, fall ill. We are not the limitless creatures we tend to imagine. But God has no such limits. He never tires, never fails. So we must turn to God for strength in our weakness. Indeed, our own weaknesses help us to see reality. We are regularly reminded that God is God and we are not by our own weaknesses, a useful and necessary lesson. If we know that He is God and turn to Him with trust and love, all things are possible. If we remain deluded that we are strong, capable people who can handle everything that comes our way, we may never turn to God and be saved. We need that balance of trust and gratitude for His gifts, and the knowledge that we are not sufficient to every challenge.

July 11

Fear not, for I am with you, / be not dismayed, for I am your God; / I will strengthen you, I will help you, / I will uphold you with my victorious right hand.
ISAIAH 41:10

When you read this, hear Jesus say these things to you. Look at the Divine Mercy Image and imagine Him speaking these words. He is, after all, the Word of God! Through the rays that pour forth from Christ's side, we are strengthened and helped; our sins are forgiven, we receive a share in the divine life, and we partake of Holy Communion. Jesus is blessing with His right hand in the Image, the very hand that had been wounded by the nail, and yet now is glorious. The Divine Mercy Image shows us the Lamb who was slain, and stands forever in the sight of God the Father. Here, truly, is the victorious Lord. Here, truly, is our strength and help.

July 12

**For I, the LORD your God, hold your right hand; /
it is I who say to you, "Fear not, I will help you."**
ISAIAH 41:13

Our faith is one long education that reality is more than
we can see with our eyes or touch with our hands. Science
tells us the same truth these days, with distant telescopes
in space transmitting to us pictures of galaxies far beyond
what we can see with the naked eye, or electron micro-
scopes showing us mysteries at the most fundamental level
of physical reality, far smaller than anything we could lay
our hands on. Whether we see it or not, the Lord God
holds each of us by the hand. We can be certain of this
because our existence depends on His love and mercy.
From moment to moment, God is choosing to love us;
He always holds us in His hands!

July 13

But now thus says the LORD, he who created you, O Jacob, he who formed you, O Israel: / "Fear not, for I have redeemed you; I have called you by name, you are mine. / When you pass through the waters I will be with you; and through the rivers, they shall not overwhelm you; / when you walk through fire you shall not be burned, and the flame shall not consume you.

ISAIAH 43:1-2

Hear Jesus say this to you! Jesus paid the ultimate price for each and every one of us, showing how deeply He loves every single person who has ever lived, or ever will live. Jesus has redeemed us all. He calls us each by name. He has bought us with His own flesh and blood. We are His, no matter what lies the devil whispers in our ear. Fear not! As God was with the Israelites when they walked through the parted sea, and the standing River Jordan; as God was with Shadrach, Meshach, and Abednego when they were thrown in the fire; as God has always been with the saints and martyrs at their worst moments, so too is Jesus with us now.

July 14

**Thus says the LORD who made you, who formed you
from the womb and will help you: / "Fear not,
O Jacob my servant, Jeshurun whom I have chosen."**
ISAIAH 44:2

God made us. We are His; He will help us. He will set
us free from the traps and the snares of the world, the
flesh, and the devil; but He is wise and good. That can
mean His help doesn't come when or how we expect it
or want it. Further, His goodness and kindness mean that
He won't spare us the painful surgery, the awful aches of
necessary physical (or spiritual) therapy. He loves us too
much to leave us in our sins. But look to the lives of the
saints for encouragement. See the peace and joy of the
martyrs. That is our final destination. That is the point of
God's law, of His loving interventions, of His providence.
To be God's is ultimate happiness. We have only to persist
in love and trust, and with His help, we can come home.

July 15

[The LORD said,] "Fear not, nor be afraid; have I not told you from of old and declared it? And you are my witnesses! / Is there a God besides me? / There is no Rock; I know not any."

ISAIAH 44:8

We may build our lives on the Lord and His promises. He will not fail us. He sets out before us in Scripture what discipleship looks like, what our call may demand. Further, the lives of His saints, apostles, patriarchs, and prophets all demonstrate that grace will be there. We are called to the impossible, and He will make all that we are called to do possible. We see that from of old; we see that across Jewish and Christian history.

The heritage of the Church bears witness to the truth of God's promises and His ability to deliver on them. We see miracles in every age, signs and wonders across the centuries.

We see the Church endure in spite of so many of us, her members, and our sins.

July 16

[The LORD said,] "Listen to me, you who know righteousness, the people in whose heart is my law; / fear not the reproach of men, and be not dismayed at their revilings."

ISAIAH 51:7

To know God is to know righteousness. To live in the state of grace is to have God's law of love within. But we are practicing Catholics, not perfect Catholics. We must remain faithful both to the law and to our repentance, to the morals taught by our Catholic faith and going to Confession when we break them. We are children of God, and we have a long way to go before we are safe home in Heaven with Him. That means that sometimes on earth, we will face "reviling" opposition to our faith and to the one to whom we commit our lives and hearts. Jesus is Lord, not public opinion. The Church is the pillar and foundation of truth, not peer pressure.

July 17

[The LORD said,] "I, I am he that comforts you; who are you that you are afraid of man who dies, of the son of man who is made like grass, / and have forgotten the LORD, your Maker, who stretched out the heavens and laid the foundations of the earth, / and fear continually all the day because of the fury of the oppressor, / when he sets himself to destroy? / And where is the fury of the oppressor?"

ISAIAH 51:12-13

Fear of the Lord is the beginning of wisdom, not fear of other people. God is God, not the strong man, the wealthy woman, or the gossips and backbiters of this world here below. God is the source of our consolation and strength, not our bank account, our ability to command other people, or the pleasures we surround ourselves with. God is always true, and the things of this world are not. Give up lesser things for God, and you shall have the One who made those things in the first place. Give up God for the sake of His creatures, and you will lose both the creatures and God. Fear of the Lord is the end of idolatry (that is, putting our ultimate trust in creatures rather than our Creator). It sets everything else in its proper perspective.

July 18

**Fear not, for you will not be ashamed;
be not confounded, for you will not be put to shame; /
for you will forget the shame of your youth, /
and the reproach of your widowhood
you will remember no more.**

Isaiah 54:4

In the days of Isaiah, children were a sign of God's blessing and favor, and to be barren was to be cursed. But again and again throughout salvation history, we see God making fertile the infertile. Abraham and Sarah have Isaac against all expectation, even when they are very old. Elizabeth and Zechariah have John the Baptist, and Mary, the Mother of God, gives birth to a Son even though she has never known man. Similarly, we call celibate men "father" and consecrated women religious "mother." God makes the Church fertile, giving birth to saved souls through the waters of Baptism, even as her priests and religious are celibate. Even when nature says a thing is impossible, for God, all things are possible.

July 19

**"Be not afraid of them,
for I am with you to deliver you," says the LORD.**
JEREMIAH 1:8

For people who are in the midst of suffering, this sort of assurance can sound glib. But it's a promise that Jesus proved true. Fidelity to God, to goodness, to faith and family may well demand everything from us. But Jesus showed us what God's fidelity means in those sorts of circumstances. When the rich and powerful people of His own day put Him to death, He suffered and died. And then He rose again. Scripture's call to us to be not afraid doesn't guarantee we will never know suffering, loss, or death. But it does guarantee that earthly, bodily death is not the end. It does promise that Jesus opens a way for us to make all suffering fruitful like His, and that death will be utterly overcome.

July 20

[The LORD said,] "But you, gird up your loins; arise, and say to them everything that I command you. Do not be dismayed by them, lest I dismay you before them."

JEREMIAH 1:17

If we are faithful to God, He will be faithful to us. If we stand by the truth, the Truth will stand by us. God can't be defeated in the long run even as we all too often experience our lives in this valley of tears as a "long defeat," as J.R.R. Tolkien put it. Even in the face of opposition and hardship, though, we are to stand by the truth. We are to abide in the household of our God, part of a nation of prophets. There's a classic phrase used to describe the prophetic power of Scripture and those who speak the Word of God: They afflict the comfortable, and comfort the afflicted. That's not a recipe for making friends with the rich and powerful on earth, but a great way to obtain lots of friends in Heaven!

July 21

[The LORD said,] "As a thief is shamed when caught, so the house of Israel shall be shamed: / they, their kings, their princes, their priests, and their prophets, / who say to a tree, 'You are my father,' and to a stone, 'You gave me birth.' / For they have turned their back to me, and not their face. / But in the time of their trouble they say, 'Arise and save us!'"

JEREMIAH 2:26-27

Israel knew better than to fall back into idolatry, and yet they did, again and again. The Chosen People had been brought out of Egypt with signs and wonders, and the sort of close relationship to God that later generations would long for. Even with that immense wealth of reasons to remain faithful to the Lord God, still they fell. The prophet here makes fun of the foolishness of their idolatry, and calls them out for being fair-weather friends of God almighty. It's a good reason to make an examination of conscience. Ask yourself: Do I pray to God and thank Him when times are good? Do I remember to make Him my first and last priority, or is He just my last priority? Do I put anything on earth before God?

July 22

Thus says the LORD: "Stand by the roads, and look, and ask for the ancient paths, / where the good way is; and walk in it, and find rest for your souls."

JEREMIAH 6:16

Our modern world is always looking for the next big thing, something better than we've ever seen before. But God came to us long ago, and comes to us today through ancient things: the Word of God in the Scriptures and the Sacraments. The moral law hasn't changed. God is as faithful as ever. So stand by the roads and look, and ask for the ancient paths. Follow Jesus, the Way. Come to know Jesus, the Truth. Live like Jesus, the Life. You will find rest for your soul. Being a Christian isn't an easy road, but it is a certain one. We know who Jesus is by reason of what He did to save us. We know the love of God, the constancy of His care, by the light in the eyes and surrounding the faces of the saints who perform the works of mercy for us.

July 23

Thus says the LORD: "Learn not the way of the nations, nor be dismayed at the signs of the heavens because the nations are dismayed at them, / for the customs of the peoples are false."

JEREMIAH 10:2

Now, all things are permissible to the Christian that are good and human. But many of the things we take for granted are neither good nor human, not in this culture of death and dictatorship of relativism. We are to be Christians, not children of our present age. What does that mean? It means, for example, that we are to know that God made man male and female, and so marriage between a man and a woman is the rightful place for marital relations. We are to be true to the entire Gospel, not just to those parts we like or find convenient. We are to welcome the fullness of truth from Christ and His Church, no matter how hard that may be.

July 24

I will make you to this people a fortified wall of bronze; / they will fight against you, but they shall not prevail over you, / for I am with you to save you and deliver you, says the LORD.

JEREMIAH 15:20

We are told to love our enemies, indicating that the Christian life doesn't allow us to escape having enemies. Indeed, as far too many saints and martyrs down through the generations have proven, being a Christian often makes you more enemies than you would otherwise have. But by the Sacraments, works of mercy, prayer, and fasting, we shall share in the strength of the Lord. We shall be able to overcome evil with good (see Rom 12:21).

July 25

"Blessed is the man who trusts in the Lord, / whose trust is the Lord. / He is like a tree planted by water, / that sends out its roots by the stream, / and does not fear when heat comes, / for its leaves remain green, / and is not anxious in the year of drought, / for it does not cease to bear fruit."

Jeremiah 17:7-8

When times get tough, it's best to be plugged into eternity. God shares His own life and love with us through the Sacraments. We can live heavenly lives here on earth. That explains the joy of the martyrs as they went to their deaths, and the impossible virtue of the saints. They weren't relying on human nature or temporal realities. They were relying on the strength that sustains the stars. Put deep roots down into God through prayer, Sacraments, fasting, almsgiving, and spiritual reading. Live deeply in faith, hope, and love. Make God your foundation, your fountain, your consolation, and no matter what comes, you will overcome.

July 26

Sing to the LORD; praise the LORD! / For he has delivered the life of the needy from the hand of evildoers.

JEREMIAH 20:13

God acts in this world in a number of ways. He sustains everything, of course, from moment to moment. He is here on earth in the Most Blessed Sacrament, and the priests and bishops stand *in persona Christi*. Jesus is present to us in the poor and the needy. But God is also present to the world in the hearts of believers. Do you realize the obligation this places upon you? We are called to be the face of Divine Mercy. We are meant to resemble Jesus, and to make His love and assistance present in the world. We must certainly pray for those in need, but we are also to help feed, clothe, house, and heal them. Do you do this? Do other people see you and find Jesus?

July 27

I will set shepherds over them who will care for them, and they shall fear no more, nor be dismayed, neither shall any be missing, says the Lord.
JEREMIAH 23:4

The prophecy is fulfilled in Christ Himself: "I am the good shepherd. A good shepherd lays down his life for the sheep" (Jn 10:11). Jesus cares for us. The Cross shows us how much. Given that the God of everything loves us that much, of what should we be afraid? Evil does not have the final say. All the rest of history is marching steadily toward the triumphant return of the God who so loved the world. Justice and mercy rule. We are given the task of redeeming the times through our joys, works, cares, and sufferings. We are offered infinite grace through the Sacraments, and given extraordinary promises with certain devotions to make our paths even smoother. The Lord God has equipped us well for battle here below. Take up your Rosary, and change the world.

July 28

For I know the plans I have for you, says the LORD, plans for welfare and not for evil, to give you a future and a hope.
JEREMIAH 29:11

Thanks to Jesus' Passion, death, and Resurrection, even the worst things that happen in the world can become means of grace. Suffering has meaning, a purpose, and can overcome all evil. God's victory in the world will ultimately be so complete that death itself is overcome for all, and all mankind will be reunited for the Last Judgment. We have ultimate hope in the face of all tragedy: hope for justice and mercy; hope that love is not just for this life, but for all time and eternity. Hope that there's meaning beyond the passage of time and the swift decay of the things we have loved.

July 29

"Then fear not, O Jacob my servant," says the LORD, "nor be dismayed, O Israel; / for behold, I will save you from afar, and your offspring from the land of their captivity. / Jacob shall return and have quiet and ease, / and none shall make him afraid."

JEREMIAH 30:10

Jeremiah prophesied the end of the Babylonian captivity, as well as its beginning. But more than that: He also prophesied the coming of a Redeemer, the greatest of all. The fulfillment of all promises comes in Jesus Christ. Therefore, the prophet could command a people being taken away into captivity to be not afraid, to be undismayed. He could tell people at one of the worst periods in their national history when it would ordinarily seem that all the Lord's promises had been broken that it was not so. Indeed, they could look ahead to a better and more perfect triumph than they'd ever dreamed of. Jeremiah could promise impossible things, and guess what? Those promises came true.

July 30

Thus says the LORD: "The people who survived the sword found grace in the wilderness; / when Israel sought for rest, the LORD appeared to him from afar."

JEREMIAH 31:2-3

The people who have been exiled from the Promised Land will see the Lord! Jesus Christ is on His way; the promises of all the covenants will be superabundantly fulfilled. Israel had a great deal to suffer, especially from the Babylonian Captivity on. When Israel sought for rest, they didn't find a mere pause in their suffering; rather, the Lord Himself was going to come. More than that: The Lord God of Israel became one of the men of Israel. God took on humanity, and specifically, Jewish humanity. Israel didn't just get a sabbath rest; they got the Lord of the Sabbath, a redeemer who would bear all burdens on their behalf.

July 31

But I will deliver you on that day, says the Lord, and you shall not be given into the hand of the men of whom you are afraid.

JEREMIAH 39:17

Trust in the Lord here is rewarded with deliverance. Fear was unnecessary. The Lord is mightier than any earthly foe, and so able to deliver us from any and all earthly foes. This, of course, leads to one of the great conundrums of the Christian faith: Why does God permit bad things to happen to good people? The answer isn't only argument or a thought, but rather the person of Jesus Christ and His Passion, death, and Resurrection. God permits bad things to happen to good people, including Himself. He has shared in our suffering; our suffering is ever present to Him. He can bring a greater good out of every evil. This may be cold comfort now in the midst of suffering, but in the end, every tear will be wiped away.

AUGUST

August 1

Do not fear the king of Babylon, of whom you are afraid; do not fear him, says the LORD, for I am with you, to save you and to deliver you from his hand.

JEREMIAH 42:11

Fear of the Lord is the beginning of wisdom, not fear of even the most powerful of earthly kings. We are summoned by Scripture to begin from a position of fearlessness when we look at the world, the flesh, and the devil, when we behold earthly power, earthly wealth, or earthly threats. Compared to God, none of them are worth a moment's concern. God can deliver us from all evil. Jesus on the Cross shows us that, sometimes, God's faithful ones must endure the worst that the world can throw at us. His Resurrection to glory shows us that all such suffering is only temporary, and will give way to eternal life.

August 2

[The LORD said,] "But fear not, O Jacob my servant, nor be dismayed, O Israel; / for lo, I will save you from afar, and your offspring from the land of their captivity. / Jacob shall return and have quiet and ease, and none shall make him afraid."

JEREMIAH 46:27

Are you in trouble and need a path forward? Anchor your life in the will of God, which is the path of wisdom and virtue. Now, that doesn't guarantee all your problems will go away. The Christian answer to a fallen world is the Crucifixion, after all, a tragedy redeemed only by the blessing of the Resurrection, of hope beyond death. Our vindication and triumph may not come in this lifetime. But the way of wisdom and virtue guarantees that your suffering will have meaning; that your life contributes to the triumph of goodness and God in the world. The Christian path is Jesus Christ Himself, and when we live in communion with Him, our whole lives open up to the light from beyond the stars.

August 3

"Fear not, O Jacob my servant," says the LORD, "for I am with you. / I will make a full end of all the nations to which I have driven you, but of you I will not make a full end. / I will chasten you in just measure, and I will by no means leave you unpunished."

JEREMIAH 46:28

The mercy of God isn't always what we expect. At times, His wrath is shown by leaving people in their sins, allowing them to be destroyed by vice and the forces of hell. Sometimes, His mercy is shown by chastisement. He stops sin by permitting His beloved to feel the consequences of our sin. But we are spared the full measure of His wrath. If we suffered as we deserved, there would be no hope for any of us. Rather, we have the logic of penance and absolution, of being forgiven our sins but also being tasked with helping heal the effects of the evil we have done. Just like physical therapy after we break bones can be painful, so too can spiritual healing and restoration cause us suffering. Healing isn't always easy, but it's worth it in the end.

August 4

[The LORD said,] "Let not your heart faint, and be not fearful at the report heard in the land, / when a report comes in one year and afterward a report in another year, / and violence is in the land, and ruler is against ruler."

JEREMIAH 51:46

Scripture shows us many things, some good, some awful. That's because the Word of God is given for all mankind, for all times and places. Those of us who are used to a stable, reliable political order may hear Scripture's talk of a divided nation, rife with violence, with ruler opposing ruler. We may wonder what relevance this has for us today. But many of our Christian and Jewish brethren have lived and endured during exactly such times. For them, this isn't a worst case scenario, a hypothetical situation; it's the reality of their daily lives. We are called to be faithful even in such extreme circumstances.

August 5

"You came near when I called on you; you said, 'Do not fear!'"

LAMENTATIONS 3:57

Sometimes, it's good to remind ourselves that God is the one who tells us to trust in Him. He's the one who sends the angels and St. John Paul II to say, "Be not afraid!" When you speak to Him, bring the promises He made. Ask Him to vindicate His promises of help and love. Persist in your prayers, as He told us to in the parable of the Persistent Widow (see Lk 18:1-8) and elsewhere. He has set Himself up for this, after all. We will only be doing what He told us to do! And listen for His response.

August 6

And you, son of man, be not afraid of them, nor be afraid of their words, though briers and thorns are with you and you sit upon scorpions; be not afraid of their words, nor be dismayed at their looks, for they are a rebellious house.

EZEKIEL 2:6

Ezekiel is being sent on a prophetic mission, one that's likely to be met with a fair amount of opposition. God is summoning him to be fearless, even as God acknowledges that Ezekiel may suffer in the process. Following God is rather like going to the gym or enduring the pains of a long journey to a wonderful destination. We need not fear anything in the world, or from the flesh, or of the devil. We need fear of the Lord, the beginning of wisdom, and that's it. And yet we will have much to endure. Can we practice this balance of fearlessness and realism? Can we acknowledge that following Christ comes at a cost, and be courageously willing to pay the price? It's only possible by the Holy Spirit. The Christian life is supernatural, after all; we will need help.

August 7

[The LORD said,] "Like adamant harder than flint have I made your forehead; fear them not, nor be dismayed at their looks, for they are a rebellious house."
EZEKIEL 3:9

God will give us the strength and virtue we need to bear all things in our Christian walk. We can't live the faith without grace. It's simply impossible. But grace comes to us as easily as an answer to prayer. We are enriched with the Word of God, with devotions, with the Sacraments, and with so much more. The fire of the Holy Spirit can temper us as fire tempers steel, strengthening us to resist all evil. If we live in the Holy Spirit, we live in love, and, "Love bears all things, believes all things, hopes all things, endures all things" (1 Cor 13:7). That is an enormous promise of power. That explains why "There is no fear in love, but perfect love casts out fear" (1 Jn 4:18).

August 8

"Can your courage endure, or can your hands be strong, in the days that I shall deal with you? I the LORD have spoken, and I will do it."

EZEKIEL 22:14

God here is promising that He shall truly punish the people in Jerusalem doing great evil. Sin, especially the sin of those who should have known better, shall not go unpunished. Here we see that the path to peace is repentance and forgiveness, while the path to destruction is unrepented sin and the sort of mercilessness that comes with envy, pride, and other unchecked sins. Fear the Lord, for He is just, but also trust in the Lord, for He is just. He takes into account ignorance, weakness, and other ways in which culpability is reduced. His Justice is the same as His mercy. His punishment heals, and His forgiveness wounds the heart, giving us the capacity to love as He loves: with blood and water, with rays of mercy pouring forth from us.

August 9

[The LORD said,] "As a shepherd seeks out his flock when some of his sheep have been scattered abroad, so will I seek out my sheep; and I will rescue them from all places where they have been scattered on a day of clouds and thick darkness."

EZEKIEL 34:12

Sheep can stop being afraid when they know the Good Shepherd is on His way. No longer will they be lost and vulnerable; rather, they will have a powerful protector and friend. We have even better hope: We know that our Good Shepherd is also our brother. He comes to redeem the rest of the family, to draw us all into the household of God. We are summoned to the great dance of giving and receiving that is the life of the Trinity, a tremendous movement of joy without end. The Lord comes to save us all, and to rescue us from the traps and the snares of the devil. He comes to free us from disordered desires, the darkness of ignorance, and the weakness of our wills. He comes with salvation and healing for all.

August 10

[The LORD said,] "They shall no more be a prey to the nations, nor shall the beasts of the land devour them; they shall dwell securely, and none shall make them afraid."

EZEKIEL 34:28

Those of us raised in a land of peace and plenty often take security for granted. It's normal, right? It's the way things are, and ought to be. What on earth is going on in places or times where they can't secure their own neighborhoods? And yet most of mankind for most of history have had to endure great insecurity, whether through want, disasters, shortages, or the evils of their own fellow men. So this promise from God sounds awfully wonderful to the rest of our brethren who read it. It's a great promise for us, as well, for money, worldly power, and earthly security are all too easily lost. But the security of God's love is eternal, if only we say yes to it and abide in faith, hope, and love, worshiping God, repenting when we sin, and helping our neighbors.

August 11

Nebuchadnezzar said, "Blessed be the God of Shadrach, Meshach, and Abednego, who has sent his angel and delivered his servants, who trusted in him, and set at nothing the king's command, and yielded up their bodies rather than serve and worship any god except their own God."

DANIEL 3:28

Our hope in God isn't just for ordinary times. Our faith, our trust in Jesus, is given to us for exactly the sort of impossible situations that Shadrach, Meshach, and Abednego had to face. They went to the fire with trust in God, knowing that they would be delivered from their captors in one of two ways: either through their deaths, or through a miracle. They were ready to face either, knowing that God is the judge of the living and the dead. He can protect us from any harm, and He can also receive us into His care when we die. Nothing puts us beyond the care of God. He is the source of the existence of everyone and everything. All that exists is loved and remembered by God.

August 12

Then Daniel, whose name was Belteshazzar, was dismayed for a moment, and his thoughts alarmed him. The king said, "Belteshazzar, let not the dream or the interpretation alarm you." Belteshazzar answered, "My lord, may the dream be for those who hate you and its interpretation for your enemies!"

DANIEL 4:19

Telling the truth to those in power can be difficult, especially when we have to share bad news. The prophet Daniel had to give the king terrible news. The king's dreams were a warning from the Lord of the madness that the king would soon suffer. Prophets are sent by God to tell us the truth, though, and so Daniel tells the king the meaning of the dream. Think of how different the world would be if more people told the truth! See how Daniel, a member of an oppressed people speaking to the chief oppressor, still wishes that such suffering be averted from the king! Remember the words of Isaiah, indicating how Jesus would fulfill His ministry: "He will not break a bruised reed / or quench a smoldering wick / until he brings justice to victory. / And in his name the Gentiles will hope" (Mt 12:20-22).

August 13

Then the king was exceedingly glad, and commanded that Daniel be taken up out of the den. So Daniel was taken up out of the den, and no kind of hurt was found upon him, because he had trusted in his God.

DANIEL 6:23

Daniel suffered being cast into the lions' den for adhering to his Jewish faith, even against the law of the king. Daniel knew true fear of the Lord. That meant he didn't fear the power of any earthly king or the danger that came from the lions. Daniel knew where true power resides. Christian courage is possible only by grace, but it comes with the guarantee that we are in the hands of God. We are in a family relationship with the most powerful being of all, and He absolutely loves us. That means that we can and should be talking to Him about the suffering we endure, bringing Him our every need and request. He will act according to His wisdom and goodness. Sometimes that resembles a dentist doing what's necessary to heal what's hurt, but other times, it means that God keeps us from every danger, even the most extreme peril.

August 14

"Fear not, Daniel, for from the first day that you set your mind to understand and humbled yourself before your God, your words have been heard, and I have come because of your words."

DANIEL 10:12

God's ways are not our ways. That means that sometimes, His will permits things to happen that we'd never want to see happen. But His wisdom is absolute; His goodness, perfect; His love, beyond measure. That means that the more we conform our minds, our wills, and our hearts to His, the better off we'll be. The better able we will be to bear life, to carry our cross, and live in the Spirit of God. So set your mind to understand: Study the Scriptures, the Tradition, and the Magisterium. Humble yourself before God: Practice regular prayer and the sacramental life. Go to Confession monthly or even weekly. Attend Mass on Sundays and Holy Days of Obligation, or even daily, if you can. Your prayers will be heard.

August 15

"O man greatly beloved, fear not, peace be with you; be strong and of good courage." And when he spoke to me, I was strengthened and said, "Let my lord speak, for you have strengthened me."

DANIEL 10:19

By such words from God can we have all the hope in the world! We are all greatly beloved by God. After all, it's His love that sustains us in existence from moment to moment. We ought to fear not, for perfect love casts out fear. God has given us His Spirit, and so we ought to be at peace. By His grace, given by His Word, we can be strong and of good courage. We can and should turn to Him in prayer, thanking Him for every gift and blessing.

August 16

I will return again to my place, / until they acknowledge their guilt and seek my face, / and in their distress they seek me.

HOSEA 5:15

Repentance is key. The only unforgivable sin would be to refuse to repent for one's sins, either out of despair, because one refused to believe in God's mercy, or out of presumption, because one refused to admit one's own sinfulness. That doesn't mean we ought to be scrupulous, that we need to be endlessly stressing out about what we might have done wrong. God loves us. He loved us before we repented, and He loves us as we walk the Christian way. But we ought to walk that Christian way with the realism that we are imperfect, practicing our faith, always with room to improve. We need to be merciful with ourselves and our Christian brethren.

August 17

Although I trained and strengthened their arms, / yet they devise evil against me.

HOSEA 7:15

Here is the contradiction at the heart of sin. We can't do anything without using the gifts God has given us. Without God, we have nothing. It was by using the gifts of God that the Roman soldiers scourged, abused, and crucified God, for example. The devil and all hell's forces are in rebellion against the source of any strength they have. Yet for all this, God continues to hold the world in existence through love. His generosity is the model for our own generosity. We are to love our enemies, pray for those who persecute us, and overcome evil with good. It's a way of life as hard as the wood and nails of the Cross, and yet as powerful as the grace that pours from the bleeding Sacred Heart of Jesus. This is the truth the devil never fathomed: to be like God is to generously share power, not to seize it.

August 18

"Fear not, O land; / be glad and rejoice, / for the LORD has done great things!"
JOEL 2:21

The people of Israel had been richly blessed with signs and wonders; we share all their heritage and more. The life of Christ is rife with miracles, and the lives of the saints stretching across two millennia are even more so. As Jesus said, "Very truly, I tell you, the one who believes in me will also do the works that I do and, in fact, will do greater works than these, because I am going to the Father" (Jn 14:12). So we have even more motives to fear not. We ought to be glad and rejoice. Study the life of Christ and the lives of the saints. Ask their help and intercession. Remind yourself of the great things God has done, and ask Him to do similar things today. He waits on our invitation, gentleman that He is, but when He moves, He moves with power at the right time in the best possible way.

August 19

He who made the Pleiades and Orion, and turns deep darkness into the morning, and darkens the day into night, / who calls for the waters of the sea, and pours them out upon the surface of the earth, / the Lord is his name.

Amos 5:8

We can take God's work of creation for granted. That's how it is with the greatest works of power. We can take for granted, for example, the incredible sacrifices of our military personnel. We don't always see all the work going on behind the scenes to protect our country. Or we assume the grocery store shelves are normally full, and will always be just as richly supplied. It takes a catastrophe to show us that huge amounts of resources and work go into the things we take for granted.

The same thing with the night sky. We don't remember that God sustains the cosmos in existence from moment to moment. But He does, every minute of every day. Our God is greater than anything we will ever confront. What, then, have we to fear?

August 20

**[Jonah] said to them, "Take me up and throw me into
the sea; then the sea will quiet down for you;
for I know it is because of me that this great tempest
has come upon you."**

JONAH 1:12

Ultimately, all our suffering here below comes from the
sins of ourselves or others, going back to Eden. Disease;
natural disasters; death — all of it was made as awful as it is
through original sin, and the sins committed ever since. Jesus
volunteered to be the one to suffer as Jonah suffered, and to
rise again as Jonah rose again from the mouth of the whale
and the depths of the sea. Our Lord shows us that the path
to peace is through repentance and penance. We can help
heal our world through our prayers, our works of mercy, our
fasting and mortification. Our good deeds (however small
they may seem or however invisible our choice to do the right
thing may feel) open the door to grace for our brethren and
the healing of the world. Wherever we let grace in, there the
light of the Second Coming begins to shine.

August 21

Then Jonah prayed to the LORD his God from the belly of the fish, saying, / "I called to the LORD, out of my distress, and he answered me; / out of the belly of Sheol I cried, and you heard my voice."

JONAH 2:1-2

Prayer reaches God the instant we say it. Wherever we are, however far we may have fallen, and however messed up our lives may be, when we begin to speak to God, He hears us. He knows us. He loves us. His grace is with us before we even open our mouths to ask for it. His love sustained us before we began to pray, and it will move in power in our lives if we persist in prayer, hope, and trust. His ways are not our ways; His timing may not be our timing. The testimony of many other people, saints and sinners, who have been in relationships with God give us proof that He does hear us and will act with power. We need to be speaking with Him in good times as well as in bad.

August 22

And the LORD God appointed a plant, and made it come up over Jonah, that it might be a shade over his head, to save him from his discomfort. So Jonah was exceedingly glad because of the plant.

JONAH 4:6

The answer to our needs may come unexpectedly. God has blessed the saints through the strangest means. He fed St. Benedict of Nursia by sending him ravens bearing bread and meat. He gave us the healing waters of Lourdes by having Our Lady ask St. Bernadette Soubirous to eat the weeds and wash in the dirt at Massabielle. God is more concerned with our salvation than He is with our pride. He is more interested in our obedience and our healing than He is our reputation or our appearance to others. So expect the unexpected as you live the Christian life.

August 23

... they shall sit every man under his vine and under his fig tree, and none shall make them afraid; for the mouth of the LORD of hosts has spoken.
MICAH 4:4

Instead of a world where a few have much and many have nothing, the prophet here promises a day shall come when everyone shall have enough, and the greed or wrath of the strong will not steal. Our Catholic faith offers us all the graces we need to find our way home to Heaven. We are given the great gifts of Catholic mystical theology and Catholic social teaching. Let us study them, practice prayer and mercy, and serve as salt and light in our earthly communities. Let us read the writings of the saints on the spiritual life and the encyclicals of the popes. Let us practice what the Church preaches, and come to the aid of those in need, both spiritually and physically.

August 24

Rejoice not over me, O my enemy; when I fall, I shall rise; / when I sit in darkness, / the LORD will be a light to me.
MICAH 7:8

A candle never seems brighter than in the darkness. The same is true of the stars. Get away from the lights of the city or the suburbs, and the skies come alive with light. Christ Our Light may be most clearly known and loved when we have been in spiritual darkness long enough for our souls to see clearly again. It may take far longer than we like for our darkness to give way to the light of God, but it will come. Saints and martyrs bear witness to that. God gives us the Divine Mercy Image as proof. Jesus comes out of the darkness, rays of grace and mercy pouring forth from His pierced side. Bring the Divine Mercy Image with you into all times and places of spiritual darkness. Welcome the light of Christ, praying, "Jesus, I trust in You!"

August 25

The LORD is good, a stronghold in the day of trouble; / he knows those who take refuge in him.

NAHUM 1:7

The goal, in the end, is to hear God say, "I know you." Why? Because God is love, and God loves those whom He knows. But He is infinitely good, and so we have a choice. We can choose whether to accept His love and knowledge of us or to turn away. But God is the source of all being, and so to turn away from His love and knowledge is to choose the outer darkness instead. To take refuge in God is to trust Him. It is to prefer Him to the outer darkness. It is to say yes to Him, however feebly, however imperfectly. Turn to the Lord, for He is good; His love and mercy endures forever. His strength is infinite, and so our hope may be infinite, as well, for He is also perfect goodness, a stronghold in the day of trouble. Even if we must suffer here below, we can be confident that justice and mercy will win in the end.

August 26

O LORD, how long shall I cry for help, and you will not hear? / Or cry to you "Violence!" / and you will not save?
HABAKKUK 1:2

We are not alone in wondering if God hears our prayers. The Scriptures are full of times when the great men and women of faith throughout salvation history have cried out to God, asking where He is and what He's waiting for. It's one of the hardest truths of the faith to hold on to in times of suffering, and yet one of the most inevitable. After all, God is infinitely wise, powerful, and loving. That means He will act for our good at the time and in the manner of His choosing. We may or may not be told anything about the time or method of His assistance coming to us. His intervention may or may not be pleasant. But be assured: He hears all prayers, wants what's best for us, and is mightier than any trial.

August 27

For I will leave in the midst of you / a people humble and lowly. / They shall seek refuge in the name of the LORD.
ZEPHANIAH 3:12

We are all called to holiness, as the Scriptures, Tradition, and the Magisterium make clear. At the same time, most of us aren't great saints. But the great saints are enormous blessings to the rest of us. The quiet sanctity of extraordinary souls such as St. Joseph or the obvious miracles of saints such as St. Padre Pio aren't just gifts for them. Their holiness and spiritual gifts are given for the benefit of the whole Body of Christ. Pray that you may live alongside great saints! They can be hard to live or work with, and yet they are such enormous gifts! Study the lives of the saints and their writings. Pray their prayers.

August 28

The LORD your God is in your midst, a warrior who gives victory; / he will rejoice over you with gladness, he will renew you in his love; / he will exult over you with loud singing as on a day of festival.

ZEPHANIAH 3:17

Our God is truly prince of peace, but He is also a God of battles. We are called to imitate Christ on the Cross, but that means we are to fight sin, death, and hell according to the wisdom, power, and love of God, not according to the ways of the world or using evil means in pursuit of a good end. The peace of the Christian is more powerful than the violence of the wicked. The long-suffering of Jesus overcomes the malice of the devil, leading to Jesus' descent into hell and triumph over the forces of evil. God is the ultimate warrior. Our faith is realistic; the world is fallen. But our help is in the name of the Lord, and so we may rejoice and be glad, even in spiritual combat.

August 29

Yet now take courage, O Zerubbabel, says the LORD; take courage, O Joshua, son of Jehozadak, the high priest; take courage, all you people of the land, says the LORD; work, for I am with you, says the LORD of hosts, according to the promise that I made you when you came out of Egypt.

HAGGAI 2:4

Courage! We don't talk about this Christian virtue nearly often enough. Courage allows us to be clear-eyed about the dangers posed to us by the world, the flesh, and the devil, while still remaining joyful. By God's grace, we can endure and overcome all. He is with us in Word and Sacrament, in the image of God in every human heart and in His sustaining work in creation. God is with us; let us always make sure we remain with Him. Let us live sacramental lives, regularly turning to God with prayer and spiritual reading, and persisting in works of mercy, in almsgiving, and love of neighbor. Let us take heart, even in the face of the challenges we face today. Let us turn to the Lord who saw the saints and martyrs through the deepest, darkest difficulties.

August 30

My Spirit abides among you; fear not.
HAGGAI 2:5

The Spirit who passed over the formless nothingness before creation and brought all things into existence; the Spirit that passed ahead of the Israelites as a pillar of cloud by day and a pillar of fire by night; the Spirit who is eternal life and perfect love, a consuming fire — that Spirit is the one that abides among the Chosen People. That Spirit is the one that came to us all at Pentecost, that dwells in the hearts of Christians in the state of grace and inspires the Church from age to age, serving as our life, our virtue, and our love. The Holy Spirit is greater than any foe or problem the Church faces, or ever will face. If the Holy Spirit is with us, then who can be against us? What have we to fear?

August 31

And as you have been a byword of cursing among the nations, O house of Judah and house of Israel, so will I save you and you shall be a blessing. Fear not, but let your hands be strong.
ZECHARIAH 8:13

Have you ever been the odd one out? Have you ever had to endure being excluded, ignored, or gossiped about by your friends, family, or coworkers? Many, many of the saints of Scripture have shared that experience. But God promises to His faithful that they shall be vindicated. Where before their name had been synonymous with a curse, now God shall make of their name a blessing. Are you having hard times? This too shall pass. Are you having prosperous times? This too shall pass. Our lives in this valley of tears traverse everything from Advent to Christmas; from Lent to Easter and Divine Mercy Sunday; from Ordinary Time to feasts and fasts.

SEPTEMBER

September 1

... so again have I planned in these days to do good to Jerusalem and to the house of Judah; fear not.

ZECHARIAH 8:15

God intends to do good things for us. That doesn't necessarily mean He will bless us with prosperity and plenty. It means that He will bring good out of evil. Through our sufferings, He will send grace. Even as the world, the flesh, and the devil assail us, we can be assured that, if we turn to Him, He will ensure that good comes out of evil. Sometimes, He alleviates our sufferings. Sometimes, He gives us grace to bear them. Sometimes, He takes what others have meant for evil and turns it to the good. How often have apparent failures turned out to be the best thing that could have happened? We didn't get the job; later, we learn what we were spared. We didn't make the appointment; later, we learn that saved our lives. When we are with God, nothing is meaningless suffering. All becomes providential, and works for good.

September 2

"I will strengthen the house of Judah, and I will save the house of Joseph. / I will bring them back because I have compassion on them, / and they shall be as though I had not rejected them; / for I am the LORD their God and I will answer them."

ZECHARIAH 10:6

Scripture is filled with God winning an apparently lost war. The elderly have children, for example; the dead rise; Israel survives, in spite of war, persecution, and every obstacle. That sort of divine intervention continues even today. The Divine Mercy message and devotion faced a ban from the Church in 1959 — one St. Faustina had foretold. And as she had also foretold, the ban was lifted. Almost 20 years later, Pope St. Paul VI overturned the ban on the Divine Mercy message and devotion in 1978. A few months later, St. John Paul II was elected pope. He would go on to beatify and canonize St. Faustina, and establish Divine Mercy Sunday. We can take all our lost causes, our fallow fields, our apostate family or friends, and bring them to God in persevering prayer. Then watch for wonders.

September 3

"I will make them strong in the LORD and they shall glory in his name," says the LORD.

ZECHARIAH 10:12

The prophet Zechariah is promising the restoration of the Chosen People. We can also read this as a promise to those of us who repent and turn again to Jesus, to the way of the Lord. It's a promise made to us all, since all of us must go to Confession at least once a year, according to the law of the Church. Our Catholic faith is realistic about our weaknesses and how prone we are to sin, but she also offers us absolution, reconciliation with God, no matter how hard or how often we fall. We have only to reach out in repentance to receive the promised strength from God. He knows we are wandering sheep in need of our Good Shepherd. He came to save the lost sheep, not to condemn us. Turn to Jesus for the grace and strength needed to live in the Spirit.

September 4

Then the clans of Judah shall say to themselves, "The inhabitants of Jerusalem have strength through the LORD of hosts, their God."

ZECHARIAH 12:5

God promises that He will make the world an enemy of His Chosen People, and that by attacking the Chosen People, the world will bring destruction on itself. That promise was attached to Jerusalem and the Jewish people, and that promise is attached to the Church and the Christian members of the Mystical Body of Christ. Where we are persecuted and attacked, we flourish. It may take generations, but it proves itself to be true in the history of the Church and in the Jewish people. After all, what sort of spiritual blindness must be present in order for people to attack the Jews, or to maliciously persecute the Church?

September 5

But as he considered this, behold, an angel of the Lord appeared to him in a dream, saying, "Joseph, son of David, do not fear to take Mary your wife, for that which is conceived in her is of the Holy Spirit; she will bear a son, and you shall call his name Jesus, for he will save his people from their sins."

MATTHEW 1:20-21

Saint Joseph is called a "just man" by Scripture (see Mt 1:19), and according to the expectations of first century Judaism, that would include a very healthy fear of the Lord. That meant that he would have recognized Mary's extraordinary sanctity. He would have believed her when she told him of the angel coming to her, of the Holy Spirit overshadowing her, and that her pregnancy was an act of God. And as a righteous Jewish man, Joseph would have known that it isn't safe to approach where God dwells on earth. As the Israelites feared to set foot on the mountain (see Ex 20:18-21), so Joseph feared to take Mary as his wife. But when God calls us, He will also equip us.

September 6

[Jesus said,] "Therefore I tell you, do not be anxious about your life, what you shall eat or what you shall drink, nor about your body, what you shall put on. Is not life more than food, and the body more than clothing?"
MATTHEW 6:25

The Gospels don't forbid us from being prudent; they forbid us from anxiety, from worry. We are to attend to the duties of our state in life; we are to see to the needs of ourselves, our families, and those entrusted to our care by vocation or by profession. We ought to live virtuously, wisely, giving measure for measure. But even when things are impossible, we are called to live the supernatural virtues of faith, hope, and love. We are called to draw on the strength given us through the Sacraments and Scripture in order to meet each moment. We are not to worry; fear of the Lord is the beginning of wisdom, not fear of hunger, thirst, nakedness, homelessness, or other evils, other privations.

September 7

**[Jesus said,] "And which of you by being anxious
can add one cubit to his span of life?"**
MATTHEW 6:27

God has provided us with the created world, and holds
everything in existence from moment to moment. We take
that for granted. Why, then, wouldn't we trust His provision?
All things come from the hands of God. If He doesn't give,
we don't have. It's true of every breath we take; it's true of
our food, our clothing, our water, our every need. All comes
from the hand of God ultimately and immediately, for nothing
exists on its own strength except for God. Everything in
creation depends on Him. If we become conscious of this, it
becomes much easier to trust Him with smaller things like our
daily bread, or a place to sleep. The Gospel and Divine Mercy
spirituality simply challenge us to choose to trust Him with
everything, and to live a life of thanks and praise.

September 8

**[Jesus said,] "And why are you anxious about clothing?
Consider the lilies of the field, how they grow;
they neither toil nor spin…"**
MATTHEW 6:28

Taking delight in beauty is a fine and blessed thing, but
putting a premium on beauty over generosity; being more
attached to our clothing than we are to the love we owe
God or neighbor, especially the needy in our community, is
a problem. We must practice a certain detachment from our
clothing, from how we look and what we wear. We need to
keep our priorities in the right order and make sure we're
spending our money according to the true importance of
things. First comes God. Next comes love of neighbor (our
families, our next door neighbors, our fellow parishioners),
and love of self (that is, taking care of one's true needs).

Then comes the non-essentials, the adornments.

September 9

**[Jesus said,] "Therefore do not be anxious, saying,
'What shall we eat?' or 'What shall we drink?'
or 'What shall we wear?'"**
MATTHEW 6:31

The lives of the saints are witness to how God fulfills the
needs of those who trust in Him. Jesus multiplied food for
the crowds who'd come to see Him a number of times.
When the first general chapter of the Franciscans took place,
St. Francis of Assisi left the provision of food in God's
hands, and behold, the townsfolk from all the surrounding
cities showed up with wagon loads of food for the holy
Franciscans. Mother Teresa of Calcutta relied on divine
assistance for her ministry to the poor, and God most abundantly provided, occasionally miraculously. Many ministries,
local churches, and individual Christians have similar stories
of the food that somehow didn't run out.

September 10

[Jesus said,] "Therefore do not be anxious about tomorrow, for tomorrow will be anxious for itself. Let the day's own trouble be sufficient for the day."
MATTHEW 6:34

How can we live this advice prudently? By framing it in the context of salvation history. The worst thing in the world has already happened. Mankind persecuted and killed God. Nothing worse can or ever will happen. Christian faith, hope, and love tells us that everything came from God, is sustained by the love and remembrance of God, and will all be assembled before God for perfect justice and mercy at the last day. That makes the rest of our lives far, far more manageable. Each day is in the hands of God, and we are not God. We are not the all-powerful Creator, but He offers to share His life and love with us, His all-powerful, all good spirit with us to assist us, to make our daily life into a participation in divinity. God offers to be with us, and so nothing will ever be greater than He on whose help we can rely.

September 11

And [Jesus] said to them, "Why are you afraid, O men of little faith?" Then he rose and rebuked the winds and the sea; and there was a great calm.

MATTHEW 8:26

Storms will come. The world isn't yet fully reconciled to God. We still live in a valley of tears, in the valley of the shadow of death. But Jesus proves here that we need fear no evil. Indeed, we only see the world, ourselves, and everything we experience in the proper perspective if we continue to abide in Christian courage. That means knowing that fear of the Lord is the beginning of wisdom, the sort of reverential fear that is the foundation of faith. God is greater than every storm. Some saints would say it's better not to ask God to rebuke the storms of life; that it's better to abide in trust, unite our sufferings to God, and remain confident that He's got everything under control. But most of us will identify with the disciples: When the storm comes, we want to wake Jesus and ask His help! Either response is within Christian tradition.

September 12

And behold, they brought to him a paralytic, lying on his bed; and when Jesus saw their faith he said to the paralytic, "Take heart, my son; your sins are forgiven."
MATTHEW 9:2

This is one of the most powerful and hopeful teachings in the entire Bible. For many of us, the gift of faith was given to us through other people. We received what has been handed on from Jesus through the apostles and their successors. We were brought to Jesus like the paralytic through the prayers of others. Sometimes, if we were baptized as babies, we were literally carried before Jesus, brought to the baptismal font in front of the Eucharistic Lord in the tabernacle and the priest who stands *in persona Christi* (in the person of Christ). And we can bring other people to Jesus with our prayers, our words, and our actions. If our neighbors have been hurt on the pilgrimage of life and lost their faith, let us make sure we're bringing them before Jesus in our prayers.

September 13

[Jesus said,] "When they deliver you up, do not be anxious how you are to speak or what you are to say; for what you are to say will be given to you in that hour ..."
MATTHEW 10:19

Many leaders on earth falsely reassure their followers that nothing will ever go wrong; that they, the leader, will always and forever control events so that their followers will always be triumphant, always be successful, always be vindicated. Jesus, the only leader with anything like the power or knowledge to actually carry through on promises like that, doesn't make those kind of promises. He assures His followers that we need to carry our crosses like Him; we will be persecuted like Him; we will be arrested and brought to trial like Him. Jesus gives us ultimate assurances of life, reward, and merciful justice; He doesn't promise lives on earth without suffering, loss, or hardship. But even as He promises suffering, He also tells us not to be afraid. By His grace, we can obey His command.

September 14

[Jesus said,] "So have no fear of them; for nothing is covered that will not be revealed, or hidden that will not be known."

MATTHEW 10:26

For those of us who have a habit of regular Confession, this can be reassuring. We have already exposed our sins to the light. For those of us who harbor deep, dark secrets that we've never willingly exposed to the light of grace in the confessional, this may be an alarming promise. But Christian realism tells us that God already knows all. Any secret we try to keep is exposed to Him. Why? Because He sustains the whole of creation in existence from moment to moment. He is present to everything. Without Him, we can't think the least thought or perform the smallest action. So trying to hide anything from God is, in itself, a failure of faith, and a failure to see reality. And at the end of time, all shall be shared with all, as Jesus says here, though seen through the perspective of perfect mercy and justice.

September 15

[Jesus said,] "And do not fear those who kill the body but cannot kill the soul; rather fear him who can destroy both soul and body in hell."

MATTHEW 10:28

Often, this passage is misunderstood. Many people assume that "him who can destroy both soul and body in hell" refers to the devil. But God is the Just Judge. The devil is merely the accuser, the prosecuting attorney. Only we, through our own actions, and the Judge, acting out of perfect goodness, justice, and truth, could ever send us to hell. So we are being told here to fear the Lord. Think of the sharp shock of fear that comes when you perceive danger for the first time, when you realize you're at the edge of a cliff or that you've had a near-miss in your car. This kind of fear helps protect us from danger, but it can't be constant, can't be nagging or pathological. Proper fear of the Lord and the sort of fear that works out our salvation with trembling (see Phil 2:12) is subsumed into love and trust of Jesus.

September 16

[Jesus said,] "Fear not, therefore; you are of more value than many sparrows."
MATTHEW 10:31

We may have some vague idea that God is very powerful, but rarely do we ever even begin to perceive just how powerful. Nothing exists without His conscious knowledge and action. Everything depends on Him from moment to moment; He sustains everything. Nothing is outside His knowledge or grasp, including each and every sparrow, on whom His eyes are always fixed. If God knows, loves, and sustains in existence the sparrows, then how much more does He know, love, and sustain us? How much more, then, can we count on His love, assistance, and provision? We usually have a straightforward confidence that we will be around in this world in five minutes, five hours, and five years. We should have even more straightforward confidence in God's love, in His care, in His power, and in His wise goodness.

September 17

[Jesus said,] "Come to me, all who labor and are heavy laden, and I will give you rest. Take my yoke upon you, and learn from me; for I am gentle and lowly in heart, and you will find rest for your souls."
MATTHEW 11:28-29

This is one of the paradoxical promises of Christ. His yoke is the cross, the path of virtue and wisdom, the straight and narrow path. It all seems very difficult. And yet it is the restful path, the lighter burden, the simpler way. The devil offers ease and comfort at the outset, then takes everything in the end, leaving us worse off than we were before. God, on the other hand, leads with the yoke, the cross, the narrow way, and in the end, we find rest, gentleness, and love. Whatever goodness we practice in our own lives will bless us and those around us in ways large and small for our lifetime and beyond. And God's grace makes impossible burdens far more bearable, and our efforts, supernaturally fruitful.

September 18

[Jesus said,] "… yet [the sower] has no root in himself, but endures for a while, and when tribulation or persecution arises on account of the word, immediately he falls away."

MATTHEW 13:21

Here we are reminded of an important truth: We can only live the Christian life by the grace of God. We are summoned to be adopted children of God, living a supernaturalized life here on earth through the Sacraments, through the study of the Word of God, through prayer, and through works of mercy inspired by the Holy Spirit, who summons us to vocations and gives us the charisms to perform them. We must have that root of grace in ourselves. Trials will come. But by the grace of God, we can overcome.

September 19

But immediately [Jesus] spoke to them, saying, "Take heart, it is I; have no fear."
MATTHEW 14:27

"My sheep hear my voice; I know them, and they follow me" (Mt 10:27). When we detect the hand of God moving in our daily lives, what consolation it can give us! Think of how wonderful and reassuring it is to approach a dangerous-looking stranger on a dark night, only to realize it's a beloved friend. But how can we recognize God's actions in the world today, or hear His voice when He speaks to us? By steeping ourselves in Public Revelation, in Scripture, and in Tradition as interpreted by the Magisterium. We can count on God's Holy Spirit to animate the Church, to preserve her, indefectible, across all the ages until the end of the world.

By listening to Divine Revelation, we can become better equipped to hear what God has to say to us today, through words, events, and other signs.

September 20

But [Jesus] turned and said to Peter, "Get behind me, Satan! You are a hindrance to me; for you are not on the side of God, but of men."

MATTHEW 16:23

Peter feared what he heard from Jesus: that the Lord would be arrested, persecuted, tortured, put to death on a cross. He was afraid for his Master, and he was afraid for himself. And so Jesus rebukes him about as sharply as Jesus ever rebuked anyone. To choose to fear the world, the flesh, or the devil isn't to be on the side of God. It's to be on the side of men. It's to make the first and biggest mistake: idolatry. Attributing to creatures the power of God is to fail to give God His due.

Only God is God; we are not. The enemies of the Church are not God, either. Neither are the powerful, the wealthy, or the gifted. If we give to creatures the reverential fear owed to God, we are a hindrance to Jesus.

September 21

**But Jesus came and touched them, saying,
"Rise, and have no fear."**
MATTHEW 17:7

When the Transfiguration happened, Simon Peter, James, and John all went flat on their faces. God in His divine splendor is a blessed sight. By His grace, we may come to find ourselves at home with holiness, but until we are perfectly purified (whether in this life or the next), being close to God can be hard to bear. But Jesus came. He touched the apostles then as He touches us today through the Sacraments and His servants, the clergy, religious, and all the saints. He speaks to us through Scripture, Tradition, and the Magisterium, through prophets, saints, and Doctors of the Church. Confronted with God, we confess ourselves sinners, and then are raised up by God to be sons and daughters. By cooperating with God's gracious love and mercy, we need have no fear.

September 22

[Jesus said,] "And you will hear of wars and rumors of wars; see that you are not alarmed; for this must take place, but the end is not yet."
MATTHEW 24:6

We often wish for this fallen world to be just comfortable enough, just perfect enough for us to not really want for anything more. And yet the Christian faith insists that the truly blessed aren't the comfortable; rather, blessed are those who mourn. Blessed are those for whom this world is not enough. Blessed are those who are not bought off by worldly comfort, or money, or earthly power, or pleasure. Blessed are we whom God permits to be troubled. Why? Because we will not make the terrible mistake of preferring our present circumstances to eternal life with God. Pray for peace, but prepare for war. Work for justice and peace on earth, but remember that until the end of the world, we will be called to carry our cross. And in spite of every earthly danger, be not afraid.

September 23

**But the angel said to the women, "Do not be afraid;
for I know that you seek Jesus who was crucified."**
MATTHEW 28:5

When Mary Magdalen and the "other Mary" found the
empty tomb and encountered the angels there, it's only
natural that they would have been frightened. But because
they were there looking for Jesus, the holy angels were their
friends. Indeed, the holy angels are friends to all who seek
Jesus who was crucified; they want to help all souls come
home to Heaven in the end. They will give a helping hand
to us in our Christian practice. All we need to do is ask.
Their assistance can be just as unexpected, just as mysterious
as God's answers to prayers, but we may absolutely rely on
the angels to hear our prayers and to act in order to help
bring about the greatest possible good in our lives.

September 24

Then Jesus said to [the women], "Do not be afraid; go and tell my brethren to go to Galilee, and there they will see me."
MATTHEW 28:10

We forget that holy things may well inspire fear. We can become so comfortable in our routine of going to Mass, receiving Holy Communion, reading the Word of God, and all the other parts of practicing the faith that we don't realize that what we are doing is awesome and even awful (in the old sense of awe!). But when the faithful women who'd followed Jesus during His earthly life encountered the Risen Lord, He had to tell them not to be afraid. Why? Mary Magdalene didn't initially recognize Him, and neither did the disciples on the Road to Emmaus. Something had changed about Him. The Resurrection of Jesus wasn't just the sort of restoration to earthly life that Lazarus and others had experienced. Jesus had risen in glory. Someday, God willing, we too shall rise again and be forever changed.

September 25

[Jesus said,] ". . . they have no root in themselves, but endure for a while; then, when tribulation or persecution arises on account of the word, immediately they fall away."

MARK 4:17

Our faith needs to put down roots in our hearts, our minds, and our very being. We need to do more than just give a verbal assent to the creed. We need to work the yeast of the Gospel into ourselves. We need be practicing Catholics, not just cultural Catholics. We need to be receiving the Sacraments according to the laws of the Church, doing regular spiritual reading of the Scriptures and the writings from our Catholic heritage, and by prayer and other works of love of God and neighbor, allowing our faith to form our lives. We need to practice making sacrifices through fasting, almsgiving, or other mortifications so that when and if we are challenged to endure tribulation or persecution for Christ, we're ready. Just as athletes prepare for the big game with exercises that, taken individually, aren't that much, so too do we prepare to finish our race strong with small works of self-denial and generosity to God and neighbor (see 1 Cor 9:24-27).

September 26

[Jesus] said to them, "Why are you afraid? Have you no faith?"
MARK 4:40

Christian courage means a well-founded trust in God that leads us beyond normal, natural earthly fears into God-given supernatural peace. Indeed, it also leads us beyond normal, natural trust! Jesus challenges His disciples here to step beyond the ordinary faith of disciples in a master, or even ordinary Jewish faith in what God would do in the world. The Incarnation was there in their holy texts, in their tradition, and in every promise that God had made to His people, but until it happened, few, if any, really saw what was coming.

September 27

But ignoring what they said, Jesus said to the ruler of the synagogue, "Do not fear, only believe."
MARK 5:36

The ruler of the synagogue has just received some of the worst possible news: His beloved daughter had died before he could bring Jesus back to heal her. Normally, that's the end. Even most of the prophets of the Lord hadn't been known to raise people from the dead. Such a wonder was rare in the extreme. And yet Jesus said to the ruler, "Do not fear, only believe." Here we are confronted with the deepest mysteries of our faith. Why the daughter of the ruler, and not our own loved ones? And yet Christian realism broadens our frame of reference beyond the boundaries of this earthly life. Simply bringing people back to ordinary earthly life means they will die again someday, whereas if they've found themselves in Heaven, they have a guaranteed eternal reward.

September 28

... when they saw [Jesus] walking on the sea they thought it was a ghost, and cried out; for they all saw him, and were terrified. But immediately he spoke to them and said, "Take heart, it is I; have no fear."

MARK 6:49-50

Many people mistake Jesus for someone to be feared, rather than the answer to every need and prayer. Yes, Jesus will come again as the Just Judge someday, but right now, we live in the time of mercy. He is walking towards us across the storm-tossed waters of history, telling us, "Take heart; it is I; have no fear." Have courage because Jesus is with us. Have courage, because God gives us the grace to have hearts of flesh on fire with the Holy Spirit, like the Sacred and Immaculate Hearts. Have courage, like the Most Chaste Heart of St. Joseph, for the Holy Spirit desires to make us His dwelling place, to share with us His grace, peace, strength, and every gift.

September 29

And Jesus said to him, "If you can! All things are possible to him who believes." Immediately the father of the child cried out and said, "I believe; help my unbelief!"
Mark 9:23-24

This is one of the most reassuring passages of all Scripture. How often do we need to pray the prayer of the father of the child? "I believe; help my unbelief!" Our weakness and the grace given us by God are on display here. We are able to pray by the Spirit of God, and we are by our fallen human nature prone to doubt. We can adapt this prayer to many other situations. "Lord, I love You; help my lack of love. Lord, I hope in You; help my lack of hope. Lord, I want what You want; help my addictions, my attachments to the things of this world, and my sins." Our weakness and sins shouldn't prevent us from praying. Rather, the more we fall, the more we need to pray. We need to bring to Jesus even our misery, even our sins. We need to give Him everything.

September 30

**And Jesus stopped and said, "Call him."
And they called the blind man, saying to him,
"Take heart; rise, he is calling you."**
MARK 10:49

God reaches out to us. We don't have to go seeking Him.
He has sent missionaries to save souls, formed disciples and
sent us to the ends of the earth to bring people to Him. He
comes to us through His Word, through the Sacraments,
through the saints and prophets. He comes to us in our
neighbor, in every moment of every day as He sustains all
things in existence. We can take heart, rise, and come to
Him because He is calling us now and always. He gives us
the strength to answer His call, and sends His disciples to
guide us, blind though we are. We have His voice speaking
to us even today and until the end of the world through the
Church and the treasures she shares with us.

OCTOBER

October 1

[Jesus said,] "And when you hear of wars and rumors of wars, do not be alarmed; this must take place, but the end is not yet."

MARK 13:7

Signs of the end clearly will be recurring features of Christian life throughout our time on earth. It is certain that Jesus will return, but we do not know when and we do not need to fear His Second Coming, as long as we are living in a state of grace. Our role is to trust. Christian courage must rise to meet every occasion, even wars and rumors of wars. Christians are meant to be characterized by joy and peace, not by fear of earthly dangers.

October 2

[Jesus said,] "When they bring you to trial and deliver you up, do not be anxious beforehand about what you are to say; but say whatever is given you in that hour, for it is not you who speak, but the Holy Spirit."

MARK 13:11

When we stick around with Jesus for long enough, we come to know that His promises are sound and worth trusting. What a promise is given here! Remember what it was like in school when you had to give a presentation. Recall all the research, the preparation, the nerves. Now imagine you're about to be questioned on your presentation by a teacher who hates you, by a hostile audience. Having to defend the faith to people who are actually persecuting the Church can be even worse. But if we are ever hauled into court over our faith, we can be at peace. We have incredible promises of help from the Lord, that the Holy Spirit who is the heart and soul of the Church will speak on our behalf. The Holy Spirit that spoke the Word of God, that speaks Jesus — that Paraclete (or Advocate) will speak to us and through us, advocating on our behalf.

October 3

But he said to [Mary Magdalene, Mary the mother of James, and Salome], "Do not be amazed; you seek Jesus of Nazareth, who was crucified. He has risen; he is not here; see the place where they laid him."

MARK 16:6

Our lives as Christians will be full of signs and wonders, if only we have eyes to see, ears to hear, and faith the size of a mustard seed. We will come before realities that are truly awesome, truly inspiring a sense of reverential fear. But that may also trigger in us alarm. We know we will have to bear crosses, that we will walk in the way of the Lord. And that may tempt us to fear, to worry, to anxiety. But alarm before one of God's wonders is out of place. Goodness and holiness isn't always comfortable; in fact, goodness in others can feel like a rebuke to us as we continue to wrestle with our attachments and our tendency toward sin. The acts of God may well throw us right out of our comfort zone. They may demand of us incredible courage, great fortitude, or heroic virtue of other sorts. If we ask for divine assistance, all things become possible. If we trust in God, the enormous treasury of divine grace is available to us.

October 4

But the angel said to him, "Do not be afraid, Zechariah, for your prayer is heard, and your wife Elizabeth will bear you a son, and you shall call his name John."

LUKE 1:13

Angels can be executors of God's wrath, as St. Faustina tells us in her *Diary* (474). So when an angel appears, until they tell you why they're there, you may well have good reason to be afraid. But consistently we hear from the angels sent by God throughout salvation history, "Be not afraid." Part of being not afraid is doing good to the best of your ability. If we're trying to be on the side of God, God's mercy will go a very long way to meet us. The angels come to help those who aim to serve the will of God. "We know that all things work together for good for those who love God" (Rom 8:28). That includes powerful, holy, terrifying angels. Thank God!

October 5

The angel said to her, "Do not be afraid, Mary, for you have found favor with God."

LUKE 1:30

Our faith offers us an incredibly high standard of holiness, one that only the Blessed Virgin Mary, out of all of us, has fully, completely, and thoroughly met. So it is consoling to read that the angel said to her, "Do not be afraid." She, the purest of the pure, the Immaculate Conception; she was told by the angel Gabriel not to be afraid. That means that our temptation to fear isn't necessarily part of our fallen human nature, but simply a relatively natural reaction to being confronted by an angel. Think of the normal human reaction, for instance, to being confronted by a bear unexpectedly, or a lion. We know instantly that here before us is something immensely dangerous, something more powerful than we are, something that we can't overcome. Now imagine discovering this apex predator is our friend, trustworthy, sent to help us. Think of the relief!

October 6

[Zechariah said,] "...we, being delivered from the hand of our enemies, / might serve him without fear, / in holiness and righteousness before him all the days of our life."

LUKE 1:74

The Christian life often doesn't look like we're rescued from the hands of our enemies. Instead, it seems to call for impossible forbearance, even in the face of oppression or evil. But we need to see with the eyes of faith and take into account the entire picture. We need to pay attention to the whole span of the life of Christ, including His Passion *and* His death *and* His Resurrection. We need to recall that we are not guaranteed perfect justice in this life, but rather the next. We need to remember that God can rescue us from beyond the grave, and that He has guaranteed He will. The ultimate tools of earthly powers have been rendered harmless; evil, suffering, and death are no longer existential threats. We are promised life eternal with Jesus. So even in the face of real persecution, of lethal threats and terrible suffering, we may serve Jesus without fear, for evil's time will come to an end and the day of the Lord will come. "Do not be overcome by evil, but overcome evil with good" (Rom 12:21)."

October 7

But the angel said to [the shepherds], "Do not be afraid; for behold, I bring you good news of a great joy which will come to all the people; for to you is born this day in the city of David a Savior, who is Christ the Lord."

LUKE 2:10-11

We are restored through the grace of God to adopted divine sonship. By grace, we may be made greater than the angels. "Do you not know that we are to judge angels" (1 Cor 6:3)? We see this clearly in Our Lady's titles: Queen of Angels; Queen of Heaven and Earth; Mother of God. So if we welcome the Divine Mercy through Baptism, Confession, Confirmation, and the Eucharist, we need not fear even the strength or the sanctity of the angels, for we are raised above them. They are our superiors by nature; we are made their superiors by grace. "So the last will be first, and the first will be last" (Mt 20:16).

October 8

Then Jesus said to Simon, "Do not be afraid; henceforth you will be catching men."

LUKE 5:10

Jesus called Simon and his brethren, fishermen all, to become apostles, proving Himself by the miraculous catch of fish. The men recognized the wonder in front of them. After all, if you're an experienced fisherman, you know that what Jesus did was a miracle! Fish where no fish could have been found; this is the same sort of miracle in nature that we see when the aged or the virgins have children, where life and sustenance is found in the desert, where God brings something out of nothing. But Jesus tells them not to be frightened by this display of divine power, for they will work greater wonders than this. They will go out to the world and become fishers of men. They will take the Good News of the Gospel to the nations, and begin a fishing expedition across the rest of human history the likes of which the world had never before seen. They would be the patriarchs of the New Israel, the Church, supernaturally fathering children through Word and Sacrament until the end of time.

October 9

[Jesus said], "As for what fell among the thorns, they are those who hear; but as they go on their way, they are choked by the cares and riches and pleasures of life, and their fruit does not mature."

LUKE 8:14

Other translations render "cares" as "anxieties." Divine Mercy spirituality centers around trust. Anxiety or worry is one of the most powerful enemies of our faith, depriving us of one of the greatest sources of grace open to us. So terrible is anxiety that it can choke the life right out of our faith, right out of our soul. We are summoned to imitate the Spirit-inspired and strengthened courage of the saints and martyrs instead. Now don't mistake this for stoicism. By our own strength, we can't possibly hold on to faith. After all, supernatural, saving faith is a gift. It must be sustained and strengthened through grace, through the Sacraments, through prayer, and through good works, especially fasting and almsgiving. We must open our hearts to ever more grace and faith, welcoming in the life and love of God, which drives out fear. "For man it is impossible, but for God all things are possible" (Mt 19:26).

October 10

While [Jesus] was still speaking, a man from the ruler's house came and said, "Your daughter is dead; do not trouble the Teacher any more." But Jesus on hearing this answered him, "Do not fear; only believe, and she shall be well."

LUKE 8:49-50

Jesus summons us beyond the ordinary faith of a student in the words of a teacher, or of a practitioner in the words of an expert. No, He asserts power over life and death the likes of which the world had never seen before. At a minimum, His contemporaries could see, He is a great prophet; but this great wonderworking prophet was also proclaiming Himself to be the Way, the Truth, and the Life. He speaks the truth, and the truth He speaks is that He is "I AM," God Himself, the Son of the Father. Jesus is mighty to save, and so what have we to fear? Nothing is beyond His power in life or in death. Where He permits evil, He will bring a greater good out of it. Respecting free will, He will at times wait for us to invite Him into problems, situations, or difficulties. A life lived in communion with Him, welcoming His power and saving grace, will include wonders.

October 11

[Jesus said], "I tell you, my friends, do not fear those who kill the body, and after that have no more that they can do. But I will warn you whom to fear: fear him who, after he has killed, has power to cast into hell."

LUKE 12:4-5

This passage is often mistaken as a warning against the devil. But the devil is only the accuser in the court of Heaven, not the Just Judge. Jesus Himself, our savior, the Divine Mercy Incarnate, is the Just Judge. Therefore, this passage is consistent with the rest of Scripture, telling us that fear of the Lord is the beginning of wisdom. We are told by Jesus not to be afraid of lethal threats. Indeed, we aren't to be afraid of anything on earth, save for the Lord Himself. And of course, as the whole arc of Scripture, of salvation history, and the Christian path of sanctification show us, perfect love casts out fear. Perfect love transforms our relationship with God. From the fall of Adam and Eve, when first we fell from adopted divine sonship, God worked through the covenant promises He made to His chosen people Israel to restore us to life in the family of God, something ultimately achieved through Jesus' Incarnation. Fear of hell becomes transformed into fear of doing evil against God. For love of God and not fear of damnation, the saints avoid sin. For love of God, we should fear no one and nothing else.

October 12

[Jesus said], "When they bring you before the synagogues and the rulers and the authorities, do not be anxious about how you are to answer or what you are to say; for the Holy Spirit will teach you in that very hour what you ought to say."

LUKE 12:11-12

The Holy Spirit will be our defender. The Spirit of Wisdom Himself will defend us against the attacks of the devil, both here on earth and in the court of Heaven. We are promised incredible grace here. What greater friend could we have in the face of the daily trials of life than the Lord and Giver of Life? Living life in the Spirit means a life open to grace and glory, a life full of miracles. If we practice a Eucharistic spirituality, a spirituality of thanksgiving, then we shall become attentive to these miracles, these graces, the moments where our practice of the Catholic faith brings good out of evil, where the Holy Spirit acts with providential power to forestall the attacks of the world, the flesh, and the devil, where even our weaknesses become opportunities for God to show His loving power and His wise goodness. Faith and prayer change the world around us. If God gives us eyes to see, we will know we have much to be thankful for.

October 13

[Jesus] said to his disciples, "Therefore I tell you, do be anxious about your life, what you shall eat, nor about your body, what you shall put on. For life is more than food, and the body more than clothing."
LUKE 12:22-23

Life is more than the necessities of life. A true teaching, and a hard one for anyone who has endured true hunger, true want, true poverty. This is why so many religious communities down through the centuries have placed such a premium on the vow of poverty. By grace, poverty and full trust in Divine Providence may be lived and lived well, since the earth and all her abundance is God's to give where He wills. As Jesus Himself proved with the multiplication of the loaves and fishes, God can and will give whatever's necessary to those who listen to His words and follow Him, even if it takes a miracle. As Jewish and Christian history has proven, that provision sometimes doesn't happen in this life, but the next; other times, the saints demonstrate God's miraculous power and provision is made in spite of natural realities. Fasting and generous almsgiving trains us in this truth, preparing us for greater tests permitted by God.

October 14

[Jesus said], "And which of you by being anxious can add a cubit to his span of life? If then you are not able to do as small a thing as that, why are you anxious about the rest?"
LUKE 12:25-26

Worry doesn't work miracles of healing. Faith and trust does, as wonder-working saints like Padre Pio have proven. Listen to his wisdom: "Pray, hope, and don't worry." That is the Christian way. Live with the words "Jesus, I trust in You," ready to meet every situation. Sometimes, we trust in Jesus to fix a situation, or to overcome some great evil. Sometimes, we trust in Jesus to help us endure, to give us the grace to abide in faith, hope, and love in spite of our weakness, in spite of the strength of the world, the flesh, and the devil. Sometimes, we trust in Jesus in the midst of deepest darkness, unable to see a way ahead, knowing only that Jesus has proven Himself trustworthy in the past, that others have been where we are now, and that we'd rather be in a time of trial with Jesus than without Him. Sometimes, we trust in Jesus as we are carrying our cross, or on the cross, or even in the tomb. Jesus doesn't tell us never suffer; never feel pain; never cry out to God in anguish. He tells us not to worry.

October 15

[Jesus said,] "Do not seek what you are to eat and what you are to drink, nor be of anxious mind."
LUKE 12:29

We begin and end life dependent on others. This should tell us something about the sort of beings we are. Mankind wasn't created by God to simply be a collection of rugged individuals, all standing on our own two feet, giving help to none and accepting no help from anyone else. Instead we come from a community, created by the Trinity, and are directed toward a community, the Church, which is the Mystical Body of Christ and the Household of God. Yes, we must work. Yes, we must use the gifts we have been given to supply for the needs of ourselves and others. Yes, inevitably we must learn a certain amount of self-reliance. But we must also learn to trust in God, to love our neighbors as ourselves, to move outside our selfishness into relationships of love and care. We must learn to receive charity with gratitude and give charity with generosity. The Trinity shows us that there is no life without love, without self-gift and openness to the gifts of others.

October 16

[Jesus said,] "Fear not, little flock, for it is your Father's good pleasure to give you the kingdom."
LUKE 12:32

The Kingdom of Heaven on earth is Jesus, and so, by extension, it's the Mystical Body of Christ, the Church. Our parishes are meant by God to be refuges from fear, from anxiety. That means we should be making our parishes into welcoming communities, into little families within the larger family of the diocese, and the great family of the universal Church. The needs of our fellow parishioners need to be treated as our own needs. Our neighbor whom we must love as our self is in the pew next to us. But our parish families are even bigger than that. We have a responsibility of love and care for all our neighbors, even those who don't believe in Jesus or who even attack the Church. What does prudent generosity tell us to do, then, to meet the needs of our neighbors out of love? Who should receive our prayer, our works, or our words of mercy? Who needs all three? And do we need to go to our parish to seek help? We should not be afraid to do so.

October 17

Being in an agony, [Jesus] prayed more earnestly, and his sweat became like great drops of blood falling down upon the ground.

LUKE 22:44

The Lord shows us how to live our lives as Christians in times of trial. The greater the suffering, the greater our prayer needs to be. Now, that doesn't mean that if we find ourselves speechless before God, we're failing to pray. Sometimes, all we can do is place ourselves physically before Jesus in the tabernacle, or a crucifix, or the Divine Mercy Image. Sometimes, all we can do is weep. But our suffering must be lived with God, not apart from Him. We should unite our sufferings with those of Jesus, and our prayers with His. We should trust Him even with our misery, our weakness, our sin. We should give Him everything, especially when our everything is at its worst. He is God; He is bearing our sins and our sufferings even now, for all the events of the Paschal Mystery are, in some sense, eternal. He can take our pain, our grief, our fury, our sorrow. He is all powerful and all-loving. Pray more earnestly the more you suffer.

October 18

[Jesus] said to them, "Why are you troubled, and why do questionings rise in your hearts?"
LUKE 24:38

These are the words of the Risen Lord. Here we have it: evidence that, even confronted by the Risen Jesus, we will usually go straight to fear and doubt. Here is proof that faith is supernatural, and fear and doubt the default state of fallen humanity. You will not remedy the loss of faith of your kids, your spouse, or your grandkids merely by admonishing them.

The appearance of the Savior to the disciples in the Upper Room had to be accompanied by soothing word and saving grace, by the gift of the Holy Spirit, in order for the most faithful of His followers to set aside fear and doubt, and begin to believe. You must pray for your family, your friends, or your neighbors who have ceased to believe. You must ask God to show Himself to them, to speak to them to assuage their fears and their doubts, just as He did for the disciples in the Upper Room. One of the best ways to do this is to share the Divine Mercy Image, either by having it blessed and displayed or by sharing blessed copies with others.

October 19

When [the disciples] had rowed about three or four miles, they saw Jesus walking on the sea and drawing near to the boat. They were frightened, but he said to them, "It is I; do not be afraid."

JOHN 6:19-20

One thing we practicing Catholics often forget is how scary holy things can be to those who aren't regularly exposed to them. Think of the awkward reverence displayed by non-practicing folks when they enter a church for a wedding or a funeral, or the trepidation with which they'll speak of things they know to be holy, not sure what to say, not wanting to offend, be blasphemous, or sacrilegious. When our ordinary existence suddenly broadens, where the natural rubs shoulders with the supernatural power of God, it's like suddenly knowing we are not alone in a darkened room. After that perfectly natural initial reaction, we are summoned to be not afraid, to rejoice and be glad in the power of God, to fear nothing and no one other than the Lord Himself.

October 20

[Jesus said], "Now is my soul troubled. And what shall I say? 'Father, save me from this hour'? No, for this purpose I have come to this hour."

JOHN 12:27

Again, it is hugely reassuring that even Jesus Himself had to come to the Father because His soul was troubled. We are not called on by God to simply be unmoved by fear. Rather, we are called to live in the Holy Spirit, in communion with God, and allow grace to strengthen us, to transform our hearts and our entire lives. We aren't forbidden from ever experiencing fear, but we are forbidden from simply remaining in fear. We must move on from natural fear, transfiguring it by prayer, Sacraments, and the Word of God from slavish fear of punishment, suffering, or death into reverential fear of God, into the determination not to do evil against the one who loves us so, or against those whom He loves. We should be like Jesus, talking to God when our soul is troubled, discerning in prayer what we are to say or do and how. We are to live our lives in the context of our relationship with God, not making the secular mistake of assuming that there are whole zones of life where God ordinarily is absent.

October 21

[Jesus said], "Let not your hearts be troubled; believe in God, believe also in me."

JOHN 14:1

Christian faith builds on natural religion (belief in God) and on the Jewish faith (belief that the God of Abraham, Isaac, and Jacob is, in a unique sense, God Almighty revealing Himself to mankind through the life of His chosen people). Now, Jesus is completing Divine Revelation in His own person. The Good News is Jesus Himself. Jesus is summoning the disciples to enduring faith, the sort that allows a person to pass peacefully through the worst dark times and tempests, just before the Passion. Jesus knows the end of the story, and is reassuring His followers that all shall be well. That's not the same thing as the promise that good will not suffer at the hands of evil. Do not let your hearts be troubled when they arrest the Rabbi; do not let your hearts be troubled when they scourge the Body of Christ; do not let your hearts be troubled when they crucify Christ and His Church. Mourn, yes, for blessed are they who mourn, but do not let your hearts be troubled, for this all has been foretold by Jesus, as well as His inevitable triumph.

October 22

[Jesus said], "Peace I leave with you; my peace I give to you; not as the world gives do I give to you. Let not your hearts be troubled; neither let them be afraid."

JOHN 14:27

We are summoned to live in peace passing all understanding, supernatural peace, graced peace. Only God's grace is sufficient for us. But God's grace can overcome all evil, all suffering, all sin. God's grace can make a way in the wilderness, see us safely through the valley of the shadow of death, and overcome anything. Again, Jesus' words here do not say that there will be no suffering. They simply say that the Christian is to abide in peace through all, live life in the Spirit through everything. Jesus shows us another way to live, one where we are certain of the love and mercy of the Father, one where, even after we cry out, "My God, my God, why have you forsaken me?" we can go on to say, "Father, into your hands, I commend my spirit." The true Gospel isn't the prosperity Gospel, but rather one signified by both Crucifix and Divine Mercy Image. The Risen Lord is wounded and triumphant; scarred and victorious.

October 23

[Jesus said], "I have said this to you, that in me you may have peace. In the world you have tribulation; but be of good cheer, I have overcome the world."
JOHN 16:33

Jesus told the disciples of the Passion to come so that they would know it was part of the divine plan, not something overcoming God. Because God is honest that His followers will suffer persecution and at times death like He did, we look on the martyrs as victors, not victims. We know that the history of the Church will mirror all the mysteries of the life of Christ: joyful, sorrowful, luminous, and glorious. We can have confidence that our God is greater than anything, for His Son rose from the dead. The power of the name of Jesus endures across time and space, proving God's promises true again and again. The Sacraments retain their power 2,000 years after the life, death, and Resurrection of Jesus. His words in the Bible convert hearts and minds, and transform the world. Jesus has conquered time and space. He has truly conquered the world.

October 24

[Peter said,] "For David says concerning him, 'I saw the Lord always before me, for he is at my right hand that I will not be shaken; therefore my heart was glad, and my tongue rejoiced; moreover my flesh will dwell in hope.'"

ACTS 2:25-26

The joy of the Lord comes through Jesus, for all grace comes through the Incarnation of God the Son. No grace is given to creation apart from Jesus, or without Jesus. With Jesus, we may hope never to be moved. With Jesus, all things are possible. With Jesus, we have peace. Fear passes away where perfect love enters in, and Jesus is the God who is Love. So welcome the Lord into your heart, your mind, and your life. Cooperate with His work of purification and sanctification. Christian courage has withstood the worst of evils; it need not fail in the face of whatever may come. The grace of God is sufficient to meet everything, if only we allow it to be. All suffering can be transformed into a powerful means of grace, if only we unite that suffering to Christ's. All that we have to endure can be faced with peace, if we let Jesus into it.

October 25

Now when [the rulers, elders, and scribes in Jerusalem] saw the boldness of Peter and John, and perceived that they were uneducated, common men, they wondered; and they recognized that they had been with Jesus.

ACTS 4:13

Here we see the vindication of Jesus' promises to His disciples. The Lord had promised that the Spirit would inspire His followers when they were arrested and brought to trial, giving them what they were to say. Now, we see that in action. The boldness of Jesus, who spoke as one with authority and not just as the scribes and Pharisees, is shared by His followers after Pentecost. We are joined by grace and Sacraments to the Mystical Body of Christ; that means we share in Jesus' life, His Spirit. When we have to bear witness to Jesus before an audience, if we open our hearts and minds in prayer to God, our words won't just be our own words, but rather the Holy Spirit will inspire us as we speak. He makes all the difference in the world, taking ordinary human words and giving them divine fire. Want to evangelize? Beg the Holy Spirit to speak to and through you, in Jesus' name and for love of God and neighbor. Turn your work and your words over to Him. He will make them supernaturally fruitful.

October 26

The Lord said to Paul one night in a vision, "Do not be afraid, but speak and do not be silent; for I am with you, and no man shall attack you to harm you, for I have many people in this city."

ACTS 18:9-10

When God calls on us to speak, it's time to set fear aside and go forth boldly, not because we are awesome, gifted, or brilliant, but because God is awesome, the giver of every good and perfect gift, and the source of all intellect. When God summons us, we should answer His call with confidence. After all, He is the one who sustains the ground beneath our feet, from whom all power or authority on earth flows. God is the source of our very existence, sustaining us from moment to moment. Why, then, would we doubt His ability or willingness to sustain us in our obedience to Him? Why should supernatural realities be any flimsier than natural realities? Indeed, the invisible angels are greater than anything visible to us here on earth. Our God is mighty to save, to sustain, to enable us to undertake whatever vocation He sets before us.

October 27

**That night the Lord stood by [Paul] and said,
"Take courage, for just as you have testified about me at
Jerusalem, so you must bear witness also at Rome."**
ACTS 23:11

Paul was arrested, but it was all in the Providence of God. God can take all things, even the choices of the people in power, and make them work for good. Oppressors do not have the final say; the wealth and power of this world does not determine our ultimate fate. God can bring good out of any evil. This can be impossible to believe on earth, as we are suffering, and yet all things are possible with God. Here, by arresting Paul and bringing him to Rome, the Roman Empire helped guarantee its own conversion, its own transformation from within. This is the logic of the Cross. The devil thought he was victorious, working through Judas and the corrupt secular and religious authorities to see to Jesus' arrest, conviction, torture, and crucifixion. But by setting all this in motion, the devil inadvertently engineered his own defeat. Similarly, the pagan Roman Empire brought Paul, one of the great promoters of the new Christian religion, to its heart, and so helped ensure that from Rome, the Gospel would go to the world till the end of time.

October 28

**[Paul said,] "I now bid you take heart, for there will be
no loss of life among you, but only of the ship."**
ACTS 27:22

Saint Paul was telling his fellow prisoners something pretty
extraordinary. They would lose the ship, something ordinarily
pretty essential to maintaining life and health at sea, and
yet no lives would be lost. This is the challenge of Christian
courage. It's not natural to keep up courage in the face of the
loss of essentials. It's supernatural. Paul had the confidence of
a man who knows that God is sending him on a mission, and
who has the gift of prophecy. When God is choosing to act
directly, our earthly prudence has to give way to supernatural
prudence, to the sort of prudence that needs grace and the
Holy Spirit to operate. Confronted by this sort of shipwreck,
we too can keep up our courage by the grace of God. Saint
Paul tells us, "For I am convinced that neither death, nor life,
nor angels, nor rulers, nor things present, nor things to come,
nor powers, nor height, nor depth, nor anything else in all
creation, will be able to separate us from the love of God in
Christ Jesus our Lord" (Rom 8:38-39).

October 29

[The angel of God said,] "Do not be afraid, Paul; you must stand before Caesar; and behold, God has granted you all those who sail with you."
ACTS 27:24

Who would have thought a prophecy of shipwreck and martyrdom would be reassuring? Yet that's precisely what we're looking at in this chapter. Because Paul knew he had to go to Rome to testify to Christ, therefore he knew that he would survive the terrible storms his ship was caught in. Because the angel of the Lord sent to him told him his shipmates would survive though they would lose the ship, he could share his reasons for hope. How strange! And yet how classically Christian. We are promised by God that we will see eternal life, if only we abide with Him. Therefore, all present storms and crosses can be taken more lightly. We know the end of the book. We've been given a glimpse of what's to come: persecution and suffering, yes, and a tomb. But in the end, all the tombs shall be empty, for all shall rise again, some to glory, others to the wages of sin. Do not be afraid. You are called to testify to Jesus before the powers and principalities of this present darkness.

October 30

[Paul said,] "So take heart, men, for I have faith in God that it will be exactly as I have been told."
ACTS 27:25

Saint Paul was not telling his shipmates to grit their teeth and gut it out, to overcome the storm and adversity with earthly strength but, rather, that grace has given them reason for hope. An angel had come to him and spoken words of prophecy. Saint Paul knew they wouldn't all have to bear present burdens for much longer. Therefore, if only they kept up their courage, they could hope to see land, and an end to their nightmare, before too much longer. In a similar way, when things get hard on earth, we know where to find light and nourishment. We have been given the Word of God in Scripture and the Eucharist. We have the safe harbor of Holy Mother Church and her teachings, a port in every storm. We have the grace of Confession to wash us clean and to resurrect us if we fall. We have the gifts and fruits of the Holy Spirit, if we ask for them and make use of them. We have prayer, devotions, sacramentals — so many treasures as Catholics!

October 31

[Paul writes,] ... we rejoice in our hope of sharing the glory of God. More than that, we rejoice in our sufferings, knowing that suffering produces endurance, and endurance produces character, and character produces hope, and hope does not disappoint us, because God's love has been poured into our hearts through the Holy Spirit who has been given to us.

ROMANS 5:2-5

How can Christians pass through the valley of the shadow of death without fear? Because we're following in the footsteps of Christ Jesus, who, as G.K. Chesterton says, knows the way back out of death. How can Christians bear sufferings with a peace and joy that draw admiration and awe from the pagan Romans? Because the Sacraments give us supernatural gifts, and the Holy Spirit dwelling in our hearts is the same Spirit that creates and sustains everything. If God gives the gifts, we may bear any burdens. So the only thing left for us to do, then, is to practice our faith. Persistence is crucial. Abiding in a loving relationship with God leads to love of neighbor and every other virtue. Love God, welcome His Spirit, and you will be transformed. You strength will be elevated to His strength; your love will be elevated to His love. Your works and words will become seasoned with salt, with the Spirit Himself. We need not fear because perfect love drives out fear.

NOVEMBER

[Paul writes], To set the mind on the flesh is death, but to set the mind on the Spirit is life and peace. For the mind that is set on the flesh is hostile to God; it does not submit to God's law — indeed it cannot; and those who are in the flesh cannot please God.

ROMANS 8:6-8

Aim for earth, and you may well miss Heaven. Aim for Heaven, and you'll get the good things of earth thrown in. Or as Jesus put it, "Seek first the kingdom [of God] and his righteousness, and all these things will be given you besides" (Mt 6:33). So set your mind and your heart on the things of Heaven, and practice the law of love. Love God, and He will be infinitely generous. Love something else as though it were God, and you will find yourself dying inside. We are made to be sons and daughters of God, not slaves of our appetites, our fears, or our needs. We are meant to be better than fallen nature, not live our lives falling for every one of the enemy's traps and snares. Love God, and you will find the good in all things. But if we reach for evil to defeat evil, or decide to solely study lies, or pursue our earthly needs above all else, we serve false gods.

November 2

[Paul writes,] For all who are led by the Spirit of God are sons of God. For you did not receive a spirit of slavery to fall back into fear, but you have received the spirit of sonship.
ROMANS 8:14-15

The heart of Christian courage is grace. We do not have to grit our teeth and shut down all emotion in order to be not afraid. No. We need to be living deep prayer lives, regularly receiving the Sacraments, and steeping ourselves in the Scriptures, Tradition, and the Magisterium. We need to be loving God and neighbor. That lived love is the root of our fearlessness, the taproot, the deepest of roots, holding us stable and strong in the face of every storm, of all temptation, of every evil. Without that deep taproot drawing from the living waters of Christ, we will fall. We will not be stronger than the world, the flesh, or the devil. Because of the Spirit of adoption, the Holy Spirit, all things are possible. Lean into your prayer life in the hard times, knowing that grace isn't always something we feel. In fact, the darker the spiritual night, all too often, the closer God is to us. Our hope is in God, not in our feelings.

November 3

[Paul writes,] I consider that the sufferings of this present time are not worth comparing with the glory that is to be revealed to us.

ROMANS 8:18

Suffering can become much more bearable if we know there's a purpose and a meaning to it. Terrible physical pain is one thing; terrible physical pain caused by medical treatment, another. So the martyrs bear witness across Christian history that, by grace, unbearable suffering becomes bearable when it's united to Christ's sufferings on the Cross. That doesn't mean we refuse ordinary medical treatment, or don't take care of ourselves. Look at the long history of Christian support of medical science, the creation of the modern hospital system, and all the works of mercy dedicated to alleviating our neighbors' suffering. But when we are confronted with unavoidable suffering, we can take it and make it a fount of grace for ourselves, the Church, our neighbors, and the entire world. This life is not all there is; we have a greater promise and a greater hope.

November 4

[Paul writes,] The Spirit helps us in our weakness; for we do not know how to pray as we ought, but the Spirit himself intercedes for us with sighs too deep for words.
ROMANS 8:26

We are reassured throughout Scripture that God comes to us out of love. God made us out of love, for love, to love in return. He wants a relationship first and foremost. That's His nature; God is Love. God is the model of family and of total, self-giving love. And His first concern with us is that sort of loving relationship. So He helps us pray. He helps us come to faith in Him, leading us along His ways toward an ever more perfect relationship of self-giving love. And our conversation with Him, our prayer lives, are an indispensable, unavoidable part of both the relationship and the transformation. So the Holy Spirit speaks for us, intercedes for us, will do wonders in our lives if we give Him any space at all.

November 5

[Paul writes,] Who shall separate us from the love of Christ? Shall hardship, or distress, or persecution, or famine, or nakedness, or peril, or sword?
ROMANS 8:35

Saint Paul is speaking the truth, a truth proven with blood again and again across Christian history, down to the present day. The love of Christ, the Holy Spirit of God, is with us, waiting to be called on. That doesn't mean that we get to control everything that happens. It does mean that we can put everything that happens into the hands of God, such that all things come to us touched by the blood of the Lamb, and therefore redeemed, becoming sacramental means of grace rather than mere suffering, death, and destruction.

November 6

[Paul writes,] Rejoice in your hope, be patient in tribulation, be constant in prayer.

ROMANS 12:12

All of this is connected, and prayer is the foundation. From prayer springs our rejoicing; we pray because we hope, and we continue to hope because we pray. We will have patience through grace, through hope, through rejoicing. Suffering will both test and strengthen us in patience. All of this builds to the sort of perseverance we need in order to abide in prayer, a conversation without end. After all, prayer on earth is a foretaste of the eternal relationship we will have with God in Heaven. Persevering in prayer means we make time in our day for regular vocal prayer, as has been modeled for us in the Church's Liturgy and Liturgy of the Hours. It means we make our Morning Offering, placing everything in the hands of God, so that our works, joys, sufferings, rest — everything becomes a prayer, becomes part of our love of God and neighbor.

November 7

[Paul writes,] I appeal to you, brethren, by our Lord Jesus Christ and by the love of the Spirit, to strive together with me in your prayers to God on my behalf ...
ROMANS 15:30

We are not alone. Never have been; never will be, no matter what the naked eye might see. God was, is, and will be with us; if He did not sustain our existence from instant to instant with love, we would cease to exist. God is always with us, always loving us. And every one of us has been assigned a guardian angel. Every one of us falls under the patronage of one or other of the saints, either through our names, our homelands, our professions, or other criteria. We are, now and eternally, in relationships of love, if only we lean into our faith. If only we remember what God has done for us, is doing for us, and will do for us, then we will know that St. Paul was doing the wisest possible thing by asking for prayer. He leaned into the communion of saints, into the loving relationships binding together the Mystical Body of Christ across past, present, and future; across life and death.

November 8

[Paul writes, God] will sustain you to the end, guiltless in the day of our Lord Jesus Christ.

I CORINTHIANS 1:8

Our own strength is not enough. Yes, God gave us gifts at the beginning of our lives. Yes, God has continued to give us gifts to the present. No, we do not have enough in those past gifts to allow us to be strong in the face of what is to come. Look at the Our Father. We pray to God in light of our weakness, our daily needs, for we ask for daily bread. We ask to be delivered from temptation and evil, for we are not God. We are not able to face all on our own strength. To be a Christian is to be somewhat pragmatic, and something of a realist. With God, all things are possible. We need Him every moment of the day simply to exist. To do the right things — well, we need even more help, especially given our concupiscence, our inclination to sin.

November 9

[Paul writes,] I want you to be free from anxieties.
1 CORINTHIANS 7:32

There's a crucial distinction running throughout the New Testament between compassionate concern for the needs or situation of others, and of worry or anxiety. We are told that those who mourn are blessed, as are the merciful. We are told we must love God and neighbor, that we need to be as innocent as doves and wise as serpents, that the path of prudence is to build our houses on the rock of Christ's teaching, of Jesus Himself. But we are forbidden anxiety or worry. We are responsible for our neighbors, our brethren, but we are not to be worried. We are called to self-giving love, to selflessness in the service of the other. We aren't to be anxious for them or for ourselves. How? Practice. Persevering prayer, the sort that feeds the Spirit within us till we pray over loaves and fishes, and we feed 5,000 people. Performing works of love, ones that teach us the true needs of others, and also how far a small gift can really go.

November 10

[Paul writes,] Be watchful, stand firm in your faith, be courageous, be strong.

1 CORINTHIANS 16:13

We are summoned to stay awake, to let the Light of Christ permeate our minds and hearts to the point where, waking or sleeping, we are in communion with God and the whole Mystical Body of Christ. Faith is the root of much else in the soul; to remain firm in the faith is to remain firm in a life of supernatural virtue, and to be practicing those virtues. Among those are courage and fortitude. You are what you love; love Jesus, and you will live and love like He does. You will have a share in the Sacred Heart, in the strength that made and sustains the heavens and the earth. You will never again be confronted by anything greater than the One who is dwelling in your heart. Christian courage isn't nature standing on its own against the world, the flesh, and the devil; Christian courage is graced nature, united to divinity through Jesus Christ, sharing in the life and love of God.

November 11

[Paul writes,] Blessed be the God and Father of our Lord Jesus Christ, the Father of mercies and the God of all comfort, who comforts us in all our affliction, so that we may be able to comfort those who are in any affliction with the comfort with which we ourselves are comforted by God.

2 CORINTHIANS 1:3-4

It's all too easy to focus on carrying our cross and assume that's all there is to being a good Christian. More self-emptying, less self-pity ... right? After all, God has already blessed us with so much, it can seem selfish or needy to ask for more. And yet St. Paul makes a vital point here: We can't give what we haven't got. Sometimes, of course, we have to do good things for other people in spite of how we feel. We have our duties to attend to. But the Christian life isn't sustainable without the Spirit and its fruits. Joylessness is a symptom worth paying attention to. A Christian without joy needs to take stock. Turn to the Sacraments and to the wise guidance of a well-educated spiritual director or confessor; take up the Scriptures, ensure you're setting aside enough time to pray, and do some of the works of mercy. Get back to the basics, because joy is one of the fruits of the Spirit. If that's missing, what else has gone?

November 12

[Paul writes, God] delivered us from so deadly a peril, and he will deliver us; on him we have set our hope that he will deliver us again.

2 CORINTHIANS 1:10

We are the inheritors of original sin, of wounds we were never intended to have to bear, of burdens God didn't mean for us to have to carry. We can't expect that we shall simply avoid peril in this life. That ship sailed with Adam and Eve. No, we can't save ourselves. We need Jesus, not just once, but throughout our lives. We need to live in a relationship with Him, and with His Church. After all, St. Paul compared the relationship between husband and wife to the relationship between Jesus and the Church. To love Jesus is to love what and whom He loves. Don't be embarrassed to ask Jesus for help. Don't let anyone, world, flesh, or devil shame you for being in a dependent relationship with God. Nothing exists without God's constant assistance, after all. The proud delude themselves; the humble are realists.

November 13

[Paul writes,] We are afflicted in every way, but not crushed; perplexed, but not driven to despair ...
2 CORINTHIANS 4:8

This is a brief statement of the whole arc of Christian history. The Church has always been blessed and burdened with the cross, always been supernaturally flourishing and always under attack from without and within. There are weeds and wheat in her, good fish and bad, till the end of time. But there is eternal fire in her core. She is alive with eternal life, so even though she die at the end of time, she will rise to eternal glory with her Spouse. So don't be afraid in times of confusion, or of persecution. Don't be afraid for the Church, for she is "afflicted in every way, but not crushed; perplexed, but not driven to despair." Thus it was in the beginning, is now, and ever shall be, till Jesus comes again.

November 14

**[Paul writes,] For this slight momentary affliction is
preparing us for an eternal weight of glory beyond
all comparison, because we look not to the things
that are seen but to the things that are unseen;
for the things that are seen are transient;
but the things that are unseen are eternal.**

2 CORINTHIANS 4:17-18

We aren't put here on earth for the sake of one lifetime, or
solely for the good works we can do during our time on earth.
We are created to be loved, and to love God in return. We are
made for grace and glory, not just this fallen nature. We are
made for eternal life and a loving relationship with the Trinity,
as well as the whole beloved family of the household of
God, which is the Church. The seeds of eternity are in every
baptized soul. That puts every temporary suffering in context.
Now, to a person who's currently undergoing their dark night
or their personal Calvary, that may sound like words easily
said and very cold comfort. It's the sort of truth that helps if
it's really internalized during the good times, but if spoken
to someone for the first time in the face of terrible grief or
sorrow, may simply sound callous. Good times and hard times
are passing; God's grace, love, and life, eternal.

November 15

[Paul writes,] ... as servants of God we commend ourselves in every way: through great endurance, in afflictions, hardships, calamities ...

2 CORINTHIANS 6:4

We are given infinite spiritual gifts in the Sacraments, in Divine Revelation, in the life and ministry of the Church. We are the wealthy, the children of the landlord, the inheritors of impossibly extensive treasures. And so when the troubles of life come, we turn to God in all our needs. We bring everything to Him, knowing there're no limit to the demands this fallen world will make on us, and there are limits to the strength of our fallen nature. Trying to muscle our way through hardship without asking God for help usually isn't maturity or virtue; it's imprudence. Only if we have been given supernatural gifts already commensurate to the challenges ahead may we find ourselves forging ahead in dryness and dust, passing through the desert on the strength of the bread of angels and the jug given from Heaven, as Elijah was given under the broom tree (see 1 Kings 19). Commend yourself, your needs, and your enemies and friends to God, and all shall be well in the end.

November 16

**[Paul writes,] I have great confidence in you;
I have great pride in you; I am filled with comfort.
With all our affliction, I am overjoyed.**

2 CORINTHIANS 7:4

Ever feel dragged down by life? Think of who we look to for
inspiration. We look to the explorers, the adventurers, the
great men of outstanding virtue or strength or talent. We are
uplifted by the achievements of our betters, and even more
so if they are our children, our kin. In sorrow, good news can
bring great joy. So in your hardships, look to the lives of the
saints and ask their intercession. The great Christians who
have gone before us have demonstrated the truth of our faith
and the power of prayer with their lives and their miracles.
They show us that grace can overmaster even the greatest of
evils, that God is love, and that love means receiving great
gifts as well as self-sacrifice. We have both the gifts of their
lives and of their intercession, of their witness and of their
worship of God. The saints are our family, deeply, truly;
they love us, and want us to join them in Heaven. Their help
is more real, more powerful, than evil or suffering.

November 17

[Paul writes,] I rejoice, not because you were grieved, but because you were grieved into repenting; for you felt a godly grief, so that you suffered no loss through us.

2 CORINTHIANS 7:9

Here is a hard truth: Sometimes, saying what needs to be said can cause sorrow in others. Now, this is a dangerous truth, for this is a classic, all-too-common excuse today. Someone is upset by my words? I only spoke the truth. Did you speak the truth in love? Did the truth spoken need to be spoken at that time and in that way? If so, then fine. But we are meant to be imitators of Jesus, who spoke soft words to the weak, sinful, and broken, and spoke harsh words to the powerful, proud, wealthy, or self-righteous.

November 18

[Paul writes,] We want you to know, brethren, about the grace of God which has been shown in the churches of Macedonia; for in a severe test of affliction, their abundance of joy and their extreme poverty have overflowed in a wealth of liberality on their part.

2 CORINTHIANS 8:1-2

By the grace of God, poverty need not be an obstacle to extreme generosity. In fact, poverty may make generosity easy. Christians are called to love God and neighbor, not money (see 1 Tim 6:10). We are meant to hold onto God tightly, not possessions or even other human persons. If we can live with a spirit of holy detachment, many of our afflictions will be much, much lighter, and our joy far greater. God is eternal; the ways of the world are not. Our present prosperity or sorrow; our present health or illness; all things here below are passing, save those things God has guaranteed, like the Church. So why not be generous? Why not be joyful? God is Lord of all. The ultimate victory has been won. All the present struggles are passing. The challenge of the Christian life isn't simply to someday attain the joy of Heaven; it's to live joyful, generous lives now, in the midst of the valley of tears, a wonder only possible by God's grace.

November 19

[Paul writes,] ... to keep me from being too elated by the abundance of revelations, a thorn was given me in the flesh, a messenger of Satan, to harass me, to keep me from being too elated.

2 CORINTHIANS 12:7

Why does God permit His beloved children, including His greatest saints, to suffer? Saint Paul gives one answer here. If he only received the gifts of God and not the burden of the cross, he would be too elated. He wouldn't be grounded; he wouldn't be humble. We are fragile creatures, and our balance is easily disrupted. Too much sorrow or too much joy is difficult to bear, this side of Heaven. Now, a man who's determined to pop our bubble may well be malicious, but God knows us better than we know ourselves. This, of course, seems to apply to one specific sort of suffering, not to all sufferings. Paul seems to be speaking of some sort of bodily affliction or abiding temptation that he has to endure, a sort of antidote to him getting a big head from all the gifts God so generously gave him throughout his life and ministry.

November 20

[Paul writes, The Lord] said to me, "My grace is sufficient for you, for my power is made perfect in weakness." I will all the more gladly boast of my weaknesses, so that the power of Christ may rest upon me.

2 CORINTHIANS 12:9

There are two things Christians may talk about with perfect confidence that will not be contradicted: the grace of God given through Jesus Christ, and our own sinfulness. God works through the weak to show who it is who is truly at work. He summoned Moses, the stammerer, to be a prophet. He gave children to the old, like Abraham and Sarah, or to the virginal, like the Blessed Virgin Mary. He proved that He was at work when He gave water in the desert, or bread from Heaven, or a pillar of fire in the dark of night. So if we are weak, thank God! Open the door to His actions through the Sacraments, through prayer, and then step out in holy boldness to do His will. He goes before us always, if we walk in His ways. All things are possible with Him, and without Him, nothing. Keep close by Him, and speak boldly of His strength and goodness, as well as your own weakness.

November 21

[Paul writes,] For the sake of Christ, then, I am content with weaknesses, insults, hardships, persecutions, and calamities; for when I am weak, then I am strong.
2 CORINTHIANS 12:10

The Christian way of life isn't the prosperity Gospel. We are not promised that all obstacles will be removed from our paths in this life, or that we will gain every success we desire. No. We are called instead to follow the martyr John the Baptist in preparing the way of the Lord. We are called to invite God in, to prepare ourselves for His Word and His arrival. Not our ways, but His ways. We must decrease so that God may increase, getting out of His way in our lives so that we may become clear crystal, allowing His light to shine to the world. And honestly, one of the easiest, quickest, and surest ways to decrease is to simply be realistic about our own weaknesses. We are reminded by our own fallen human nature and the fallen world in which we live that God is God and we are not on a daily, sometimes minute-by-minute, basis.

November 22

[Paul writes,] For [Christ] was crucified in weakness, but lives by the power of God. For we are weak in him, but in dealing with you we will live with him by the power of God.

2 CORINTHIANS 13:4

We can't expect lives without suffering if we follow Jesus, He who died on a Cross. We can't expect to be among the mighty of the earth, the richest of the rich, the biggest names. We can't expect it, but it may happen. Think of Mother Teresa. She was faithful to the mission Jesus gave her through all spiritual darkness, all suffering, all obscurity. And because she was faithful, she ended up being handed fame and global honors. She didn't need any of that, but it came anyway, largely because she held it so lightly, largely because she was an authentic Christian, serving the poorest of the poor for love of God and neighbor. But oh, how much she suffered! How much she bore for love of God and neighbor! We can do the same but only by the grace of God. In this vale of tears, we can count on burdens, and by grace, they may become blessings.

November 23

**[Paul writes,] For [Christ] is our peace,
who has made us both one, and has broken down
the dividing wall of hostility …**
EPHESIANS 2:14

Earthly divisions may give way to grace. It's our job as
Christians to pray and work for that to happen, welcoming
in Jesus Christ, He who bridges all divides. After all, there
is no greater gap than the difference between divinity
and humanity, and yet in Jesus, that divide is overcome.
Through Jesus, then, all divisions between humanity may
be transfigured. As all are sons and daughters of Adam and
Eve, so now are we all intended to be sons and daughters of
the New Adam and the New Eve, members of the family of
God, brethren of Jesus and Mary. We are called to be sons
and daughters in the Son of God. In Him, enemies become
friends. Let us make sure we are fervent in obtaining the
graces necessary to overcome evil with good, with Jesus,
through prayer, fasting, and almsgiving, through the
Word of God and the Sacraments.

November 24

[Paul writes,] Finally, be strong in the Lord and in the strength of his might.

EPHESIANS 6:10

Here is the secret of the saints. The Church has survived and thrived, not by human strength, worldly wealth, or earthly power, but rather by her saints, by those of us who have truly been "strong in the Lord and in the strength of His power." God is almighty; the world, the flesh, and the devil all have limited power. God is eternal; everything in creation has a beginning and an end. If we are strong in the Lord, then we are infinitely strong, as strong as He makes us. There then is nothing we can't overcome. This is why we remember the Roman martyrs in every Liturgy, but not the Roman emperors. This is why the world knows the name of Joan of Arc, but not the names of the kings who battled, or the names of the clerics who condemned her. This is why, even though the Nazis and the Communists came to control Poland after St. Faustina's life, they have both passed into history, but Faustina's work is alive and spreading throughout the world.

November 25

**[Paul writes,] Most of the brethren have been
made confident in the Lord because of my
imprisonment, and are much more bold to speak
the word of God without fear.**

Philippians 1:14

The result of Paul's imprisonment, ironically, was to ensure
he was more able to spread the Gospel, not less. He wrote a
number of his letters from prison, after all, and bore witness
through his arrest to the Gospel, to constancy in the face of
suffering, to the grace of God. This is the science of the Cross,
the secret of Christianity. We follow a God who became man,
who suffered, died, and was buried — and who rose again.
The Church is never stronger than when she is persecuted.
The Gospel never spreads farther or faster than when they kill
the proclaimers, plant us in the ground like seeds, and water
us with the blood of the martyrs. We are bearers of a Word
that will not return to God void. It seems impossible from a
worldly perspective, and yet this is the history of Christianity.
We suffer more evils as a result of luxury or corruption than
we do as a result of attack.

November 26

[Paul writes,] It is my eager expectation and hope that I shall not be at all ashamed, but that with full courage now as always Christ will be honored in my body, whether by life or by death.

PHILIPPIANS 1:20

Saint Paul is modeling evangelization here. It's not about us. It's about Jesus. It's not about the messenger. It's about the message. Now, our eager trust in God is an important part of that message. We can't give what we haven't got, after all. But ultimately, the Word will be preached whether I am alive or dead. God wins, whether I have done my duty or not. My success or failure is in the hands of God, under His control. He permits me to play a role in the proclamation of the Gospel, but He does not need me. So there is an end to my fear. There is an end to any anxiety that I may not be good enough, or that my work may be fruitless. Some sow, others reap. Jesus is Lord. It is better for me and for the brethren if I preach, and preach well, but it is not indispensable. Christianity frees us from having to be the Creator, from having to be in complete control.

November 27

[Paul writes,] I am the more eager to send [Epaphroditus], therefore, in order that you may rejoice at seeing him again, and that I may be less anxious. So receive him in the Lord with all joy, and honor such men, for he nearly died for the work of Christ, risking his life to complete your service to me.

PHILIPPIANS 2:28-30

Christians have always especially honored our missionaries and our martyrs. We know that proclaiming the truth of Jesus Christ is both a blessing to those who hear it and also is a threat to the world, the flesh, and the devil. Jesus and all those who've served Him didn't live without enemies, but loved those enemies. Serving Jesus means living and loving like Jesus. It means recognizing we aren't at home in this fallen world, that life in the valley of tears is life in the shadow of death. It also means learning Christian courage, having no fear ultimately of either tears or death. Blessed are those who mourn, for we shall be comforted. Blessed are those who are persecuted for the sake of Jesus, for we shall have our reward.

Be what He has called us to be, and be fearless. We are salt and light. We are His hands and feet. Remember that the nails will pierce His hands and feet, but those same hands and feet rose again imperishable.

November 28

[Paul writes,] Have no anxiety about anything, but in everything by prayer and supplication with thanksgiving let your requests be made known to God.

Philippians 4:6

We are to pursue what we need, but we are to do it in peace, calmly, without worry, all while speaking to God. He is the source of all the things we need, after all, and whether we are aware of it or not, we depend on Him from moment to moment for our very being. He can take care of all our other needs, but He does tend to wait to be invited into situations before taking an active role. Intercession makes all the difference in the world because human free will makes all the difference in the world. God, in order to create freely loving creatures, has had to limit Himself and His interventions. Christians lift those limits by persevering, loving, trusting prayer. Prayer swings the door open. Sticking with prayer swings that door all the way open, and sometimes breaks down the wall between Heaven and earth altogether. Prayer can make a place or a time holy; it can make God all in all.

November 29

[Paul writes,] The peace of God, which surpasses all understanding, will guard your hearts and your minds in Christ Jesus.

PHILIPPIANS 4:7

Saint Paul was famously concerned with Christian morals, with fidelity to orthodoxy, with obedience to Jesus Christ in a world that couldn't care less about Him or His followers, unless the world was killing them. And yet he keeps on hammering away about the peace of God, passing human reason, that should abide in the hearts and minds of Christians. We who live today should take note, and draw deep on the sources of grace given us by Christ and His Church to similarly be at peace.

November 30

[Paul writes,] I know how to be abased, and I know how to abound; in any and all circumstances I have learned the secret of facing plenty and hunger, abundance and want. I can do all things in him who strengthens me.

PHILIPPIANS 4:12-13

Saint Paul wasn't kidding. He'd endured a lot in the service of the Gospel. So what he says here wasn't just encouraging words from a pastor, trying to steady his flock. He'd lived what he described. Further, the blood of the martyrs and the steadfast, persevering apostolate of the evangelists continues to prove Paul's advice across Christian history. How could St. Lawrence, the Deacon, joke as he was tortured? How could St. Thomas More go with good humor to be beheaded? How could martyrs across the centuries sing hymns and psalms as they went to their deaths? "For man it is impossible, but for God all things are possible" (Mt 19:26). There can be joy, even on the cross.

DECEMBER

[Paul writes,] Over all these put on love, which binds everything together in perfect harmony. And let the peace of Christ rule in your hearts, to which indeed you were called in the one body. And be thankful.

COLOSSIANS 3:14-15

Christians are not called to fear this wicked world, or the many temptations and falls to which the flesh is prone, or the devil and his forces. We are called to be characterized by peace, founded on fear of the Lord, perfected by love, and coming from trust in God. We are meant to be salt, light, a city set on a hill, dwelling in a house built on rock. Are you characterized by peace, or by fear? Are you confident in God, or fearful of worldly powers and the enemies of the Church? No enemy of the Church is more powerful than Jesus. Good is greater than evil, now and into eternity. Clothe yourselves with love of God and neighbor, and be at peace.

December 2

[Paul writes,] You yourselves know, brethren, that our visit to you was not in vain; but though we had already suffered and been shamefully treated at Philippi, as you know, we had courage in our God to declare to you the gospel of God in the face of great opposition.

1 THESSALONIANS 2:1-2

We are given great grace through the Sacraments, through the Scriptures, through our prayers and devotions, and through our fasting and almsgiving. The graces we receive help us on to even greater works, greater flowering of the living faith within us. With God, all things are possible. It's that grace that empowers us to proclaim the Gospel in season and out of season with our lives and our words, not our own natural strength or talents. Saint Paul was a man of deep prayer, and so a man of supernatural strength. With God, we can be at peace. We need not be afraid. Many evangelists and servants of the people of God have shown the same supernatural fortitude across Christian history.

December 3

[Paul writes,] We sent Timothy, our brother and God's servant in the gospel of Christ, to establish you in your faith and to exhort you, that no one be moved by these afflictions. You yourselves know that this is to be our lot.

1 THESSALONIANS 3:2-3

It's easy to make the same mistake as St. Simon Peter, who wanted to avert the Passion of Jesus (see Mt 16:22). Who wants to suffer persecution, or watch loved ones suffer? And yet we were promised by Jesus that to follow Him is to suffer as He suffered (see Jn 15:18-25). We are to take up our crosses and follow Him (see Mt 16:24). So we know that suffering comes with following Jesus, that the Church will abide through the same sort of persecution as her Head. We need to be strengthened and prepared by the Gospel, by grace, by the Sacraments and the whole life of the Church. We also need to be at peace. Remember, we are forbidden from worry or anxiety, but encouraged to bring all things to God in prayer.

December 4

[Paul writes,] Since indeed God deems it just to repay with affliction those who afflict you, and to grant rest with us to you who are afflicted, when the Lord Jesus is revealed from heaven with his mighty angels in flaming fire, inflicting vengeance upon those who do not know God and upon those who do not obey the gospel of our Lord Jesus.

2 THESSALONIANS 1:6-8

We may not see justice in this life, but we know that the Just Judge will have the last word at the end of time. Pray for mercy now, both for yourself and for your enemies! (see Mt 5:44-48). Pray so that enemies may become brethren. Pray so that the fire of divine love will head off the fire of divine justice. But don't be afraid of the wickedness of the world, of all the ways that the just suffer at the hands of the unjust. Mourn the evils of this world, yes; serve truth, justice, love, Jesus; pursue righteousness in this world, yes. All these things are declared blessed by Jesus. But don't be afraid of the powers and principalities of this present darkness. If we are true to Jesus and trust in His love, we are the light of the world; we need not fear the dark.

December 5

**[Paul writes,] But the Lord is faithful;
he will strengthen you and guard you from evil.**
2 THESSALONIANS 3:3

We are all too often weak, all too often unfaithful, disobedient, or even addicted to our vices. God is good; left to our own devices, we are not. But God does not leave us in our sins. He came to find us, to heal our wounds and resurrect our souls. Jesus is the Good Shepherd, come to find us, His lost and straying sheep. We can look forward to life eternal with Him, an infinite giving and receiving of love and life forevermore. We begin here and now in the Eucharist, receiving Him, Body, Blood, Soul, and Divinity, a shadow and a foretaste of the eternal exchange in Heaven. God is good, and so we may be made good once more. God is true, and so we may come to live the truth rather than a lie. God can be counted on, and so we too may come to be pillars of faith and virtue.

December 6

**[Paul writes,] I remind you to rekindle the gift of God
that is within you through the laying on of my hands;
for God did not give us a spirit of timidity but a spirit of
power and love and self-control.**

2 TIMOTHY 1:6-7

When we were baptized and confirmed, God gave us gifts,
indelibly marking our souls and sealing us in the Holy Spirit.
But we do need to rekindle those gifts. We do need to spend
time in prayer, listening to the Word of God, and living out
God's love in the world through worship and works of mercy.
We do need to go to Confession, washing ourselves clean of
sin with the blood of the Lamb and the fire of the Holy Spirit;
we do need to be receiving the Eucharist regularly. We do
need to persist in the Sacraments, prayers, and good works,
especially if we are struggling with some habitual sin or failing.
"Above all, maintain constant love for one another, for love
covers a multitude of sins" (1 Pet 4:8).

December 7

[Paul writes,] Now you have observed my teaching, my conduct, my aim in life, my faith, my patience, my love, my steadfastness, my persecutions, my sufferings, what befell me at Antioch, at Iconium, and at Lystra, what persecutions I endured; yet from them the Lord rescued me.

2 TIMOTHY 3:10-11

Are you suffering? Look to saints with similar lives as you. Other members of the Body of Christ have endured all sorts of evils here in this valley of tears. We can ask them for their intercession, trusting that they will recognize and sympathize with our plight. Certainly we may or may not have miraculous help with our problems, but if we don't open the door to Heaven's intercession with our prayers, we're liable to find ourselves trying to bear impossible burdens on our own strength. We were intended for a very different, unfallen world. It's not weakness or failure to have to reach out to God and neighbor for help. It's only to be expected. Indeed, that's why Jesus came!

December 8

[Paul writes,] The Lord stood by me and gave me strength to proclaim the word fully, that all the Gentiles might hear it. So I was rescued from the lion's mouth.
2 TIMOTHY 4:17

The proclamation of the Gospel has power. Doing the will of God has power. We need to be abiding in prayer and the sacramental life, studying the Word of God and the teachings of His Church, and worshipping and doing works of mercy. All these things open doors to the Holy Spirit in our hearts, minds, and lives. All these things contribute to us shining in the world, radiant with the light of Christ. It's a gradual process for many of us with plenty of trips and stumbles along the way, but a practicing Catholic is like a burning candle: gradually, there's less of us and more light. By the grace of God, we may hope to become light through and through, to join the saints in Heaven.

December 9

[Paul writes,] Since therefore the children share in flesh and blood, [Jesus] himself likewise partook of the same nature, that through death he might destroy him who has the power of death, that is, the devil, and deliver all those who through fear of death were subject to lifelong bondage.

HEBREWS 2:14-15

Death remains a curse and a heavy cross to bear in this life, no doubt about it. And yet we have the promise of the Resurrection to tell us that death has fundamentally lost its power. Death is a parting, not a permanent loss. Since God is outside of time, we may pray now for our loved ones both dead and alive. We may hope to help them say yes to God so that, at the end of their lives, they welcome Jesus as savior and friend, going to be with Him forever. No matter what, we know we shall see all of mankind at the resurrection of the dead, the Last Judgment. Death, therefore, is no longer the conclusion to anyone's life. Rather, it's a door to a different way of existence. Christians need not fear death, as the saints and martyrs have proven.

December 10

[Paul writes,] Let us then with confidence draw near to the throne of grace, that we may receive mercy and find grace to help in time of need.

HEBREWS 4:16

God isn't tired of hearing from you. Remember, He is eternal; all of time is before Him simultaneously, in a way we can barely begin to imagine. He will not wear out. His love will not come to an end. He is love, and therefore, His love is eternal. Bring your needs to God. Come to Him with confidence, again and again. That's what He told us to do in the Gospels. He gave us the model of the persistent widow bugging the unjust judge for justice, for instance, or the neighbor who comes pounding on the door late at night needing to borrow some food. Persist in prayer! Do what God told us to do! Not every prayer receives a yes, but all prayer opens the gates to Heaven's help and intervention.

December 11

[Paul writes,] In the days of his flesh, Jesus offered up prayers and supplications, with loud cries and tears, to him who was able to save him from death, and he was heard for his godly fear.

HEBREWS 5:7

Here is the central paradox of Christianity: Jesus begged for the cup to pass from His lips, for the coming suffering to pass from Him, but left it in the hands of the Father as to what would come. So Jesus suffered — and rose from the dead. His prayer was heard; His suffering and death was overcome by glory. God's answer to our prayers may not come in this life; it may well come when it seems to be too late. God may answer our prayers when any answer seems to be impossible. Sometimes, our reunion with our loved ones will be on the other side of death. Sometimes, the victory of good over evil comes at the Last Judgment. Our faith isn't just for this life, and Christ's power isn't confined to what we know or understand.

December 12

**[Paul writes,] Do not throw away your confidence,
which has a great reward.**
HEBREWS 10:35

Abide in your confidence in Christ, even when your doubts
seem most compelling, or your fears seem all too real. Abide
with Jesus, and wait on the Lord. Saints across the whole
arc of Christian history prove that great rewards come from
trusting in God, and that much may be lost if we give up faith
or hope. It is love that makes this possible, God's love for us
and our love for Him. We need grace to hold on; the greater
the burden, the greater our prayer needs to be.

December 13

[Paul writes,] By faith [Moses] left Egypt, not being afraid of the anger of the king; for he endured as seeing him who is invisible.
HEBREWS 11:27

What Moses saw by faith, Simon Peter saw with his own eyes: Jesus, walking on water, calling him on. When you've got your eyes fixed on Jesus, the anger of earthly powers is a secondary consideration. There are more important things than wealth, power, or pleasure; more important things than Pharaoh's wrath, your boss' ire, or anything earthly. True prophets like Moses follow the way set before them by God, and sometimes that way leads across water, through walls, or over buildings. Follow the way of the Lord, and the impossible will become possible. It can take some time, prayer, and practice at our faith before we can do the same, but if God calls us, it is all possible.

December 14

[Paul writes,] For time would fail me to tell of Gideon, Barak, Samson, Jephthah, of David and Samuel and the prophets— who through faith conquered kingdoms, enforced justice, received promises, stopped the mouths of lions, quenched raging fire, escaped the edge of the sword, won strength out of weakness, became mighty in war, put foreign armies to flight.

HEBREWS 11:32-34

We don't believe solely because some ancient text makes a bunch of claims about God. We believe because there have been believers before us, and there are believers around us, who burn bright with faith and grace. Look at the last century alone: Faustina Kowalska, Maximilian Kolbe, Fulton Sheen, Padre Pio, John Paul II, Mother Teresa, and many more. There are people across the history of Judaism and Christianity through whom God shone like the sun, and like the sun, transformed what He shone on. We look at the lives of the saints and we see the humanly impossible. We see heroic virtue and world changing faith, hope, and love. We see grace transfiguring their lives, and through their lives, the rest of the world as well.

December 15

[Paul writes,] Consider [Jesus] who endured from sinners such hostility against himself, so that you may not grow weary or fainthearted.

Hebrews 12:3

Remember Jesus and His Passion: **"There is more merit to one hour of meditation on My sorrowful Passion than there is to a whole year of flagellation that draws blood; the contemplation of My painful wounds is of great profit to you, and it brings Me great joy"** (*Diary*, 369). If they treated Jesus like this, why should we be surprised when we encounter hostility or opposition? If we unite that suffering to the Cross of Christ through prayer, offering it all to the Father in union with Jesus at Mass, it can become a fount of incredible graces and contribute to Jesus' saving work. We are offered a way forward even through hell on earth; not an easy road, but a road. And a road out of hell is better than being trapped!

December 16

[Paul writes,] We can confidently say, "The Lord is my helper, / I will not be afraid; / what can man do to me?"
HEBREWS 13:6

This can be a useful verse to memorize and pray throughout the day, especially in times of danger. We do live in a world of both Cross and Resurrection, of both suffering and miracles; that paradox abides. It can be very frustrating and make it hard to trust. And yet there are no miracles without trust, only suffering. Better a world with miracles than one without. Better to suffer with Jesus than without Him. Better to abide in trust and love of God and neighbor than to give up hope. But of course that sort of supernatural trust and love depends on the grace of God; Christian courage is itself a miracle. So hand everything over to God, be not afraid, and ask Him for what you need.

December 17

Count it all joy, my brethren, when you meet various trials, for you know that the testing of your faith produces steadfastness. And let steadfastness have its full effect, that you may be perfect and complete, lacking in nothing.

JAMES 1:2-4

As we practice our faith, we grow in all sorts of ways. Grace heals and perfects our fallen human nature. As we place in God's hands the impossible burdens of life in a fallen world, we are able to rest, to recover, to gradually heal from the effects of our sins and the sins of those around us. Following Jesus allows us to make all things sources of grace for us rather than burdens or curses. Trials become crosses, the source of grace for us and the whole world. We are called to apply the science of the saints so that we become as innocent as doves and wise as serpents.

December 18

**Is any one among you suffering? Let him pray.
Is any cheerful? Let him sing praise.**
JAMES 5:13

One of the most consoling realities about Scripture is that it contains many, many laments from the people of God to the Lord in Heaven. We are not summoned to fake a cheerful face when things have gone badly. Jesus Himself wept when Lazarus had died, and begged the Father in the Garden of Gethsemane to spare Him suffering. We can and must do the same! Complain, but do not complain *about* God; complain *to* God with full faith and trust in His love and power. Conversely, if we are cheerful and feeling blessed, we are not forbidden from our songs of praise. We are encouraged to share our joys and sorrows alike with God.

December 19

In [the promise of salvation] you rejoice, though now for a little you may have to suffer various trials, so that the genuineness of your faith, more precious than gold which though perishable is tested by fire, may redound to praise and glory and honor at the revelation of Jesus Christ.

1 PETER 1:6-7

Those saints and martyrs who persevered to the end now celebrate with God in Heaven. The modern world dismisses such hope as "pie in the sky by and by," but that's the equivalent of the grasshopper making fun of the hardworking ants who are preparing for winter. Just because a good thing must be worked and waited for doesn't mean it's worthless now. Our ability to "delay gratification" to sacrifice lesser goods now for greater goods later, is a hallmark of the successful, and no one is more successful than the saints. No reward is greater than God Himself, given to those of us who give ourselves to Him.

December 20

Sarah obeyed Abraham, calling him lord.
And you are now her children if you do right
and let nothing terrify you.
1 PETER 3:6

Do what is good, and fear nothing. Trust in the Lord's promises. Trust in the gifts given to us by God, and the assurance that if we turn to Him in every need, we shall be given what His wisdom and goodness determine. Rejoice in the Lord and the gifts He gives to us, for gratitude is wisdom, and the heart of Christian spirituality. Remember that the Eucharist (Thanksgiving) is the source and summit of our faith. Remember also that in the household of God, we are called to lay down our lives for each other.

December 21

But even if you do suffer for righteousness' sake, you will be blessed. Have no fear of them, nor be troubled, but in your hearts reverence Christ as Lord.

1 PETER 3:14-15

Jesus has reset our whole scale of dangers and rewards. We aren't to live as our neighbors live, where this life is the boundary of our expectations. We aren't to have the natural human priorities of pleasure, safety, or wealth. We are meant to be living for God, and therefore loving our neighbors as ourselves, as God loves them. We have a new set of goals with the hope of eternal life with Christ. We know that whatever short-term harm may come as a result of doing good is nothing compared to the glory to come. We know that no earthly good is worth losing our souls. Therefore, we do not fear what our neighbors fear. We do not behave like citizens of the world, but like citizens of Heaven.

December 22

Since therefore Christ suffered in the flesh, arm yourselves with the same thought, for whoever has suffered in the flesh has ceased from sin, so as to live for the rest of the time in the flesh no longer by human passions but by the will of God.

1 PETER 4:1-2

We were told by Jesus to take up our crosses and follow Him. Usually, that's a reference to the trials and temptations of daily life, but sometimes, to do what is right is to embrace our cross in a rather more literal way. Our model in this should be the martyrs who suffered for Christ and His Church, and the saints who offered up their physical sufferings in union with Christ's Passion in order to obtain spiritual treasures. If we love God and neighbor even to the point of remaining faithful through suffering, we will be living our earthly life no longer by human desires, but by the will of God. We will have transcended fallen human nature and participated with grace in rising to new life in the Spirit, becoming true living members of the Body of Christ.

December 23

Humble yourselves therefore under the mighty hand of God, that in due time he may exalt you. Cast all your anxieties on him, for he cares about you.
1 PETER 5:6-7

In this age of self-promotion, belief in the power of positive thinking, and selfies, turning to humility first seems wrong. Yet the Christian tradition is unanimous about the vital importance of humility. Pride is the worst of the seven deadly sins, intrinsic in some way to all sin, since sin at its most basic is prioritizing our own judgment, our own needs and wants, or our own goals over the will of God. Humility sets us free from the delusion that we are in control, that we have sufficient power, wisdom, or virtue to overcome the world unaided.

Have the humility to be under the law, and therefore the protection, of God. Give Him all your anxieties, knowing He is God and you are not. Your earthly challenges are not God, either. God loves you. Be not afraid.

December 24

[Peter writes,] And after you have suffered for a little while, the God of all grace, who has called you to his eternal glory in Christ, will himself restore, establish, and strengthen you.

1 PETER 5:10

One of the most hopeful parts of Scripture is the message that suffering is temporary. God's grace opens the path to Heaven for all, if only we respond to that grace and cooperate with it. That means that there's an end in sight for even the worst of situations. Also, God promises tremendous graces to us through prayer, the Sacraments, and living the Christian life, graces that can make suffering here on earth more bearable or even alleviate it entirely. No matter what, our suffering can be joined to the suffering of Christ on the Cross. We can offer it up and open the floodgates of Heaven's graces to the needs of ourselves and our neighbors on earth. We are members of the Body of Christ, and when the Body of Christ is crucified, the world is saved.

December 25

To those who have obtained a faith of equal standing with ours in the righteousness of our God and Savior Jesus Christ: May grace and peace be multiplied to you in the knowledge of God and of Jesus our Lord.

2 PETER 1:1-2

Our faith makes possible our peace. We know where all came from (God who is love) and we know where everything is returning (God who is love). Knowing God is to discover the two foundational truths that lead to conversion: God loves us absolutely, and we are sinners in need of a savior. Our repentance and return to right relationship with Him through His Church is to become peaceful; as we pray and study the Word of God, coming to know the Father and the Son, we also come to know the love they share, the Holy Spirit, and come to participate in the peace surpassing all understanding. All this comes to us as a gift from God, Goodness Itself, Righteousness Itself.

December 26

I write to you, fathers, because you know him who is from the beginning. I write to you, young men, because you are strong, and the word of God abides in you, and you have overcome the Evil One.

1 JOHN 2:14

You can't love what you don't know, and ultimately, you can't know what you don't love. We are commanded to love God, and so we must know Him. We must read the Word of God, receive the Sacraments given us by God through His Church, and come to Him in prayer. Further, we must love what and whom God loves. We must love our neighbors, and our enemies. We must do works of mercy for them, overcoming evil with good. We must imitate the love and mercy of the saints, like St. Faustina, St. Dominic, Blessed Bartolo Longo, Mother Teresa, and so many more extraordinary witnesses to the Divine Mercy of God. By grace, we can be strong enough to love, forgive, and be merciful.

December 27

**There is no fear in love, but perfect love casts out fear.
For fear has to do with punishment,
and he who fears is not perfected in love.**
1 JOHN 4:18

Fear of the Lord is the beginning of wisdom. Here at last is
the end, the goal, of wisdom. Here is the secret sought by
philosophers, lived by married couples, and sealed by the Holy
Spirit in every Christian heart, if only we are open to the grace.
Fear of the Lord remains one of the gifts of the Holy Spirit,
and it retains its importance as an antidote to idolatry, but in
the heart of the sons and daughters of God, it is never again
the fear of a slave toward a master. It is instead the loving,
reverential fear of a son toward a good and patient father, the
fear of failing the beloved. When we love God as we are meant
to do, we are no longer afraid of His punishment, but of
His disappointment, of the pain our sins cause Him.

December 28

**When I saw [Jesus], I fell at his feet as though dead.
But he laid his right hand upon me, saying,
"Fear not, I am the first and the last, and the living
one; I died, and behold I am alive for evermore, and I
have the keys of Death and Hades."**
REVELATION 1:17-18

Here is the difference grace makes. When our human nature,
marred by sin, is confronted with the awesome holiness of
God, we fall flat. We are as nothing before Him. But by grace,
we are adopted sons and daughters of God. We are friends
with the Almighty, invited into His household, made a part of
His family. By grace, then, we can have Christian courage. We
need not be afraid. We are given supernatural life, supernatural
gifts. With those, we can look at God without fear. We can
face the Power from whom all other power comes. Of what
else would we ever need to be afraid? This is the fount of the
courage of the martyrs, the impossible bravery of missionaries
and evangelists across the centuries. Gaze upon Jesus, the face
of the mercy of the Father, and take heart.

December 29

[Jesus said,] Do not fear what you are about to suffer. Behold, the devil is about to throw some of you into prison, that you may be tested, and for ten days you will have tribulation. Be faithful until death, and I will give you the crown of life.

REVELATION 2:10

This may sound impossible. After all, Jesus is promising us martyrdom. He's talking about prison, and suffering, and all sorts of awfulness. How can we not be afraid? This is possible by grace, by the Sacraments, and by prayer. We are summoned to turn to God in every need, to accept the charity He gives us both directly and through our loving brethren. We are meant to be humble Christians. By the grace of God, we may overcome every temptation from the devil. By the grace of God, we may be faithful unto death, and receive the crown of life.

December 30

**"Who shall not fear and glorify your name, O Lord? /
For you alone are holy. / All nations shall come and
worship you, / for your judgments have been revealed."**
REVELATION 15:4

In the end, we return to the beginning of wisdom: fear
of the Lord. Again, fear of the Lord isn't meant to be the
dominant or overriding characteristic of our relationship
with God, but it is a basic virtue, a foundational virtue.
Why? Because it puts everything and everyone else in
context. We are reminded by fear of the Lord that we are
not the almighty, the Creator. Further, fear of the Lord
is the beginning of wisdom because it tells us not to fear
anyone or anything else. God is almighty, not the world, the
flesh, or the devil. Fear of the Lord holds us in reverence of
God, preventing us from falling into idolatry of any of His
creatures. Why should I fear anything that is lesser than the
God who loves us all? Of what or whom should I be afraid?

December 31

I [John] heard a great voice from the throne saying, "Behold, the dwelling of God is with men. He will dwell with them, and they will be his people, and God himself will be with them; he will wipe away every tear from their eyes, and death shall be no more, neither shall there be mourning nor crying nor pain any more, for the former things have passed away."

REVELATION 21: 3-4

One day, our Lord promises, all struggles, sorrow, and suffering will end. God will "wipe away every tear." All of creation will be made new, and there will be complete healing, overflowing grace, and everlasting glory. The joy of Heaven defies human description, but St. John's inspired words, along with visions of the saints, partially lift the veil for us. Saint Faustina writes, "Today I was in heaven, in spirit, and I saw its inconceivable beauties and the happiness that awaits us after death. I saw how all creatures give ceaseless praise and glory to God. I saw how great is happiness in God, which spreads to all creatures, making them happy; and then all the glory and praise which springs from this happiness returns to its source; and they enter into the depths of God, contemplating the inner life of God, the Father, the Son, and the Holy Spirit, whom they will never comprehend nor fathom" (*Diary, 777*).

INDEX OF IMAGES

About the Author

Father Donald Calloway, MIC, a convert to Catholicism, is a member of the Congregation of Marian Fathers of the Immaculate Conception. Before his conversion to Catholicism, he was a high school dropout who had been kicked out of a foreign country, institutionalized twice, and thrown in jail multiple times.

After his radical conversion, he earned a B.A. in Philosophy and Theology from the Franciscan University of Steubenville, Ohio; M.Div. and S.T.B. degrees from the Dominican House of Studies in Washington, D.C.; and an S.T.L. in Mariology from the International Marian Research Institute in Dayton, Ohio.

He is the author of 18 books, including the international bestseller *Consecration to St. Joseph: The Wonders of Our Spiritual Father* (Marian Press, 2020) that has been translated into more than 25 languages. He currently serves as the Vicar Provincial and Vocation Director for the Mother of Mercy Province.

Father Calloway leads pilgrimages to Marian Shrines around the world. Find out more at FatherCalloway.com

To learn more about Marian vocations, visit
Marian.org/vocations

or visit Fr. Calloway's website,
FatherCalloway.com

Further Reading from Marian Press

DIVINE MERCY CATHOLIC BIBLE

Divine Mercy is a gift given to us by God. Devotion to Divine Mercy has been growing through the revelations to St. Faustina and the modern-day ministry of St. John Paul II. Many Catholics may not realize that the revelation of Divine Mercy is interwoven into the Bible. Throughout the Bible, moments of mercy shed light on the Sacred Scripture's message of God's infinite love for us. The *Divine Mercy Catholic Bible* clearly shows the astounding revelation of Divine Mercy amidst the timeless truths of Sacred Scripture. This Bible includes 175 Mercy Moments and 19 articles that explain how God encounters us with mercy through His Word and Sacraments. 1712 pages. Y111-BIDM

EUCHARISTIC GEMS
DAILY WISDOM ON THE BLESSED SACRAMENT
Y111-EUGM

SACRED HEART GEMS
DAILY WISDOM ON THE HEART OF JESUS
Y111-SHGM

MARIAN GEMS
DAILY WISDOM ON OUR LADY
Y111-MGEM

ST. JOSEPH GEMS
DAILY WISDOM ON OUR SPIRITUAL FATHER
Y111-SJEM

Call 1-800-462-7426 or visit FatherCalloway.com

More Inspiration from Fr. Calloway

CONSECRATION TO ST. JOSEPH
THE WONDERS OF OUR SPIRITUAL FATHER

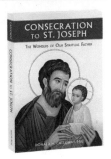

In the midst of crisis, confusion, and a world at war with the Church, it's time to come home again to our spiritual father, St. Joseph. In this richly researched and lovingly presented program of consecration to St. Joseph, Fr. Donald Calloway, MIC, brings to life the wonders, the power, and the ceaseless love of St. Joseph, Patron of the Universal Church and the Terror of Demons. Paperback. 320 pages. Y111-FCSJ

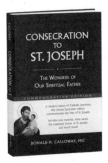

CONSECRATION TO ST. JOSEPH
COMMEMORATIVE EDITION

A beautiful hardbound premium edition of *Consecration to St. Joseph* to commemorate the incredible Year of St. Joseph. Includes a new foreword, 3 ribbons for marking pages, full-color artwork, and lots of other special new material. This will definitely be a keepsake to treasure! 320 pages. Y111-HCJO

CONSECRATION TO
ST. JOSEPH FOR CHILDREN AND FAMILIES

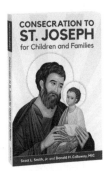

Protect your family! Entrust your family to St. Joseph. Why? Because God Himself did. God entrusted the Holy Family to St. Joseph to keep them safe, and so should you. Drawing on the wealth of the Church's living tradition, Fr. Donald H. Calloway, MIC and co-author Scott L. Smith, Jr., call on all of us to turn to St. Joseph, entrust ourselves, our children and families, our Church, and our world to our spiritual father's loving care. Watch for wonders when the Universal Patron of the Church opens the floodgates of Heaven to pour out graces into your family's lives. Y111-CJHB

Call 1·800·462·7426 or visit FatherCalloway.com

More Inspiration from Fr. Calloway

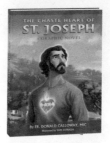

THE CHASTE HEART OF ST. JOSEPH
A GRAPHIC NOVEL

How much do you really know about St. Joseph? He was once a little boy and played like all children. He had royal blood, and could have been a king. He was a young man when he married Mary. He was a wonderful father to Jesus. He was the brave and steadfast protector of the Holy Family. He's the model of manhood. He's worked many miracles and is a powerful intercessor for us … And he had a pure, chaste heart. Join Fr. Calloway as he tells the dynamic and inspiring story of St. Joseph, our spiritual father and the "Terror of Demons." You'll learn that, whenever you need help, just "Go to Joseph!" Hardcover. 84 pages. Y111-JOEG

NO TURNING BACK: A WITNESS TO MERCY
10TH ANNIVERSARY EDITION

In this edition, Fr. Calloway looks back in a new introduction to this perennially powerful witness to the transforming grace of God and the Blessed Mother's love for her children. His witness proves a key truth of our faith: Between Jesus, the Divine Mercy, and Mary, the Mother of Mercy, there's no reason to give up hope on anyone, no matter how far they are from God. Paperback. 288 pages. Includes photo section. Y111-ANTBK

UNDER THE MANTLE
MARIAN THOUGHTS FROM A 21ST CENTURY PRIEST

Father Calloway deftly shares his personal insights on topics including the Eucharist, the papacy, the Church, Confession, Divine Mercy, prayer, the Cross, masculinity, and femininity. The Blessed Virgin Mary is the central thread weaving a tapestry throughout with quotes about Our Lady from saints, blesseds, and popes. Paperback. 300 pages. Y111-UTM

The Rosary is Mary's Prayer

CHAMPIONS OF THE ROSARY
THE HISTORY AND HEROES OF A SPIRITUAL WEAPON

Tells the powerful history of the Rosary, a spiritual sword with the power to conquer sin, defeat evil, and bring about peace. Endorsed by 30 bishops from around the world! Paperback. 428 pages. Y111-CRBK

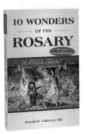

10 WONDERS OF THE ROSARY

The Rosary is presented here in all its wonder: leading armies into battle; defeating the enemies of Christ and His Church; and transforming hearts and minds in order to save societies and entire civilizations. Paperback. 192 pages. Y111-WOND

THE ROSARY SPIRITUAL SWORD OF OUR LADY DVD

Father Calloway explains the power of Our Lady's favorite devotion, the Rosary, in this engaging DVD based on his internationally renowned talks. Y111-RDVD

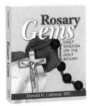

THE HOLY ROSARY
Meditations and colorful art accompanying every mystery of the Rosary. 64 pages.
Y111-THRB • Spanish: Y111-THRS

PRAY THE ROSARY DAILY
A complete guide to praying the Rosary. Y111-PR2

ROSARY GEMS
DAILY WISDOM ON THE HOLY ROSARY
Y111-RGEM

Call 1-800-462-7426 or visit ShopMercy.org

The Marian Fathers of Today and Tomorrow

What are you looking for in the priests of tomorrow?

- ☑ Zeal for proclaiming the Gospel
- ☑ Faithfulness to the Pope and Church teaching
- ☑ Love of Mary Immaculate
- ☑ Love of the Holy Eucharist
- ☑ Concern for the souls in Purgatory
- ☑ Dedication to bringing God's mercy to all souls

These are the top reasons why men pursuing a priestly vocation are attracted to the Congregation of Marian Fathers of the Immaculate Conception.

Please support the education of these future priests.
More than 30 Marian seminarians are counting on your gift.

Call: 1-800-462-7426
Online: Marian.org/helpseminarians

Join the
Association of Marian Helpers,
headquartered at the
National Shrine of The Divine Mercy,
and share in special blessings!

**An invitation from
Fr. Joseph, MIC, the director**

**Marian Helpers is an Association of Christian faithful of the
Congregation of Marians of the Immaculate Conception.**

By becoming a member, you share in the spiritual benefits
of the daily Masses, prayers, and good works of the
Marian priests and brothers.

This is a special offer of grace given to you by the Church
through the Marian Fathers. Please consider this opportunity
to share in these blessings, along with others whom you
would wish to join into this spiritual communion.

**The Marian Fathers of the Immaculate Conception of the
Blessed Virgin Mary is a religious congregation of nearly 500
priests and brothers around the world.**

Call 1-800-462-7426 or visit Marian.org